W9-BUG-705

LI ZHENSHENG · RED-COLOR NEWS SOLDIER

A CHINESE PHOTOGRAPHER'S ODYSSEY
THROUGH THE CULTURAL REVOLUTION

Edited by Robert Pledge

Li Zhensheng's text adapted from interviews by Jacques Menasche

Additional text by Jacques Menasche

Introduction by Jonathan D. Spence

RED-COLOR NEWS SOLDIER

LI ZHENSHENG

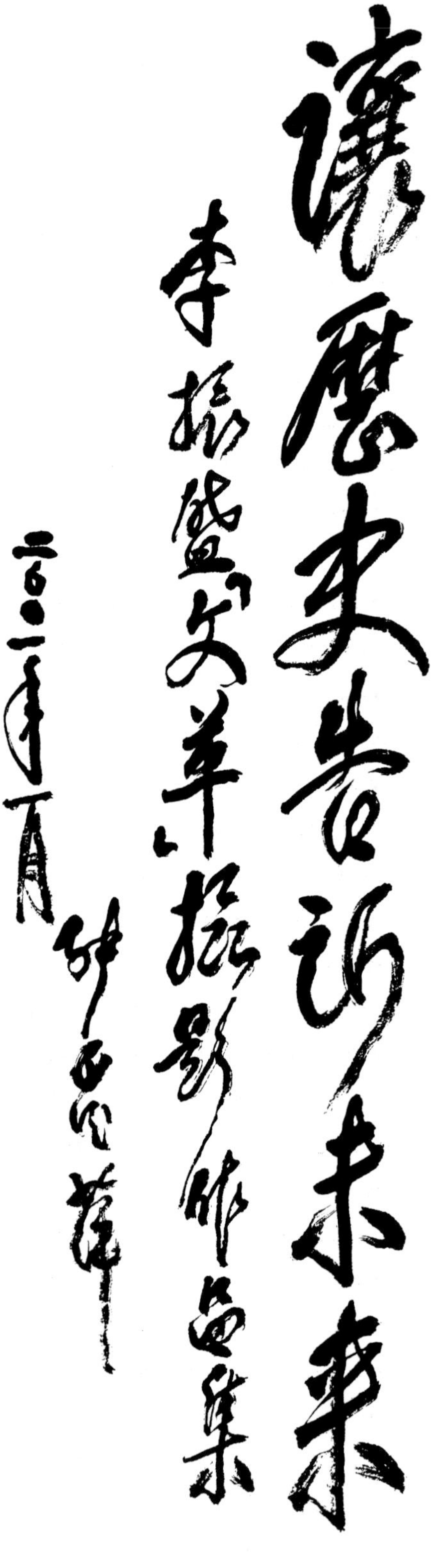

让歷史告訴未来

李振盛文革攝影作品集

二〇〇一年夏 張爱萍書

Calligraphy by General Zhang Aiping, former Vice Premier and Defense Minister: "Let History Tell the Future. Li Zhensheng's photography book on the Cultural Revolution"

6

Red-Color News Soldier is the literal translation of the four Chinese characters printed on the armband first given to Li Zhensheng and his rebel group in Beijing at the end of 1966, eight months after the launch of the Great Proletarian Cultural Revolution. There are other, more fluent translations, but none retains the musicality of the four character words brought together.

For a long time in the Western world, Mao Zedong and the Cultural Revolution were perceived with amazement and fascination; only very rarely with horror. In the late 1960s and early 1970s, rioting students around the world were inspired by the finger-pointing, slogan-shouting style of the Red Guards, and Andy Warhol in New York was producing his renowned silk-screen paintings of Mao, the "Great Helmsman." Even today, all the chaos of that period can seem somewhat romantic and idealistic in comparison with the contemporary Chinese society we see and hear about.

With this in mind, it was necessary to produce a clearer and more truthful image of the turmoil that turned China upsidedown during the Cultural Revolution. Li Zhensheng was the one person who, through his exceptional photographic legacy, could convey this truth on the printed page. A few guidelines were established up-front with Li's agreement: none of the photographs would be cropped; the images would be presented in the most accurate chronological order possible so as to best depict the historical process; and precise captions would accompany the images, with facts verified through additional research and double-checked against the archives of the *Heilongjiang Daily*, where Li worked for eighteen years.

Over a period of several years, Li delivered to the offices of Contact Press Images in New York approximately thirty-thousand small brown paper envelopes bound together with rubber bands in groups according to chronology, location, type of film, or other criteria that changed over time. Each envelope contained a single negative inside a glassine pouch. Some of these had not been removed since Li had cut them from their original negative strips and hidden them away thirty-five years earlier. On each envelope Li had written detailed captions in delicate Chinese calligraphy. Communes and counties, people's names, official titles, and specific events were all carefully noted. Yet as Li's written account clearly demonstrates, his memory of the period is still clear and detailed.

For three years, from 2000 to 2003, a small group including Li, translator Rong Jiang, writer Jacques Menasche, and I (and later to be joined by Li's daughter Xiaobing) met nearly every Sunday to collectively piece together this history of a largely unknown era. In these exhausting and, at times, animated sessions, we pored over a variety of archival and scholarly documents, conducted interviews, reviewed images, and even listened to Li sing revolutionary songs from the time.

During the period of the Cultural Revolution the whole of China became a theater in which the audience was increasingly part of the play—from the poorest peasant attending a "struggle session" to the "class enemy" forced to bow at the waist in humiliation; from the rarely seen leader waving from a Jeep to the denounced and the denouncers; from the rebels to the counterrevolutionaries, the Red Guards and the old guard all played their roles. With armbands and flags, banners and big character posters, and Little Red Books turned into props, the stage was dominated by the inaccessible star, surrounded millions of extras, some shouting, some silenced.

But thanks to Li, seemingly anonymous faces and places take on names and identities. Li shows the surreal events to be all too real. Through his lens, these people and occurrences from so far away are made at once personal and universal, and all too familiar, reminding us of events in Chile, Rwanda, Bosnia, Afghanistan, and Iraq. The Cultural Revolution unleashed the frustration and anger of a new generation eager to change the world, but the force was harnessed and used by those in power for a decidedly different purpose: its own complete domination. In the late 1960s, student riots erupted in other cities on other continents, but they never resulted in the same premeditated violence initiated by those at the helm of the Chinese state.

We will be forever grateful to Li for having risked so much to doggedly preserve the images in this book at a time when most of his colleagues agreed to allow their negatives to be destroyed. Li was a young man in search of himself, as seen in his many self-portraits in this volume, who wished to leave behind a trace of his own existence as well as his dreams of individuality and a better world. History is indeed Li Zhensheng's paramount concern and this book's main purpose: to remember and revisit those haunting and tragic events that were the Great Proletarian Cultural Revolution.

Robert Pledge

A peasant activist leads a crowd at a
rally during the Socialist Education
Movement in the countryside of
Heilongjiang province. 12 May 1965

INTRODUCTION

Li Zhensheng: Photographer for a Time of Troubles

by Jonathan D. Spence

It is a basic belief of most historians, including myself, that the more time elapses after an event has taken place, the easier it is going to be to interpret that particular event, and to understand it. In the case of the Cultural Revolution in China, which brought misery to the country for the whole decade between 1966 and 1976, that generalization ceases to have any meaning. To the contrary, the more time has passed, the harder it has become to make sense of one of the most catastrophic and complicated mass movements and political upheavals ever to afflict China. Was this the last flailing attempt of Mao Zedong to stamp his revolutionary vision on the nation he had come to control? If so, how did he relate his own cult of personality to the strictures of Communist Party discipline? Was he even aware of the consequences of his words and his actions? Were those politicians, especially those gathered around Mao's wife in Shanghai, acting out their own cynical scenarios, or did they truly believe the extraordinary things they were saying about their former comrades? How was it that so many millions of the young — both boys and girls — were caught up in the rhetoric of Mao's deliberate appeal to the forces of disorder? How did individuals in responsible positions in the Party bureaucracy so swiftly yield to slogan-chanting teenagers? From what source did the wellsprings of youthful violence emerge, and what was the rationale that led individuals to justify the vicious and often fatal punishments, beatings, and humiliations that they inflicted on their elders? And even if they could justify that violence, what inner justifications did they have for the pitched battles that they fought against other so-called revolutionaries from within the students' ranks?

If we are one day truly to be able to answer such questions and to gain an understanding of not only their personal motivations, but also the hidden meanings of the Cultural Revolution, it may well be because of the evidence provided by witnesses such as the news photographer Li Zhensheng. In many thousands of rolls of film, shot between the mid-1960s and the early 1980s, Li tracked the developments of the Cultural Revolution in China's northernmost province of Heilongjiang, in and around the city of Harbin. As an official photographer for a state-controlled newspaper he was, of course, to some extent doing no more than obeying orders in framing his photos; but as a young man with an acute eye, he was also achieving something far more complex: he was tracking human tragedies and personal foibles with a precision that was to create an enduring legacy not only for his contemporaries, but for the generations of his countrymen then unborn. And as Westerners confront the multiplicity of his images, they, too, can come to understand something of the agonizing paradoxes that lay at the center of this protracted human disaster.

Harbin, the focal point of Li's Cultural Revolution images, is a new city by the standards of China's long history. It grew initially in the late nineteenth century as a communications hub, deliberately located at the point where the newly built Chinese Eastern Railway (financed with Russian government money to provide a shorter route to Vladivostok than the more northerly Trans-Siberian railroad) crossed the Sungari River. Within a few years, the fledgling city was connected by further railway development to a southern Manchurian railway system that led to Mukden (and thence to Beijing) as well as to Korea. Despite the bitterly cold winter climate, the new town grew swiftly, as Japanese investment was added to Russian and as Chinese settlers poured into the region to take advantage of the access to the rich mineral, timber, and grain resources of the region that Harbin now provided. During the 1930s and 1940s, Harbin developed further under Japanese rule and became one of the major cities in the short-lived Japanese-controlled state of Manchukuo. In the later 1940s, after a brief period of Soviet Russian occupation at the end of World War II, Harbin became the center of the communist base area, from which China was successfully unified under communist control in 1949. As the capital of Heilongjiang under the communists, Harbin grew to be a city of over two million, and became the major political and industrial center of the northeast. As a result of this combination of factors, the Communist Party and military bosses of Manchuria played major roles in Beijing's planning for the whole country's future in the period after the initial victory, and in the mid-1950s were also to be subjected to some ruthless purges.

For many years before the outbreak of the Cultural Revolution in 1966, while Li was still in school, China had been becoming acclimatized to mass movements of various kinds. These had included mass rallies against the United States' involvement in the Korean War; huge protests against the Americans' alleged use of germ-warfare toxins in Manchuria; the marshaling of entire rural communities in the name of land reform; assaults by the entire population against natural "pests" such as birds, rodents, snakes, and insects; attacks on urban "capitalists" and on those who had worked with foreigners; mass criticisms of writers and artists for deviating from the standards of socialist realism and descending into cultural revisionism; and campaigns against bureaucrats who were unable to transcend their personal interests and to work selflessly for the socialist state. In late 1958, these many campaigns were subsumed under an even greater revolutionary banner, that of the Great Leap Forward: this pushed the nation onto the path of rural and industrial self-reliance by means of the institution of people's communes. These were designed as immense centralized rural communities that would draw together the disparate realms of agriculture, local industry, defense against foreign aggressors, child-raising and cooking, health care, and cultural production. Within a few years, the communes had proved to be a disastrous failure, posited on hopelessly unrealistic projections of growth that exhausted both the people and the land and culminated in a catastrophic famine that spread across rural China from 1959 to 1962.

It was on the ashes of those ruins that Mao, with the help of trusted generals in the People's Liberation Army, began to construct the edifice of a new structure of revolutionary change. The Great Proletarian Cultural Revolution, as Mao came to envision it, would once and for all erase every trace of political "revisionism" and bureaucratic backsliding and render impossible the restoration of capitalism, by summoning to the fray the revolutionary energies of the entire society, from the youngest to the oldest. No one would be spared the winds of change, and life would be transformed. Education would focus on the values of agricultural and industrial production alone, and conventional schools and colleges would be closed. A new social and revolutionary force, the Red Guards, would spring forth from this liberation of energies and would apply themselves to the destruction of the old order, old thinking, old habits, old artifacts. Unhampered by the inherent conservatism of local governments, they would be free to implement whatever change they saw as necessary in the name of Chairman Mao.

This was the world that Li was deputed to capture with his camera as he started his new job as a photojournalist for the *Heilongjiang Daily*, the leading newspaper in Harbin. Usefully for us, his photographic record started in 1964, so that from his first images we can get at least some sense of the campaigns against the United States' "imperialist" involvement in Vietnam, and the public struggle sessions of 1965 against local farmers branded as "landlords" that were already part of the regional experience of the time. The huge scale of these rallies is well observed, as are the shabby garments and the careworn looks of those adjudged to be the capitalists of the countryside. The depictions of summary justice are juxtaposed with Li's equally careful images of the "correct" political attitudes, as manifested in militia drills, local elections for Party representatives, workers dutifully chanting their carefully prepared Maoist texts, and — presiding over all — the omnipresent face of Mao.

Though we know now that many of the preparations for the Cultural Revolution had been under way in Shanghai and Beijing from early in 1966, we can see from Li's photographic record how the tides of revolutionary rhetoric and action only began to truly affect Harbin in mid-August of that year. Without attempting to repeat here the names and official positions of all the key actors, it is perhaps enough to emphasize that Li's meticulously documented details of those August events are an invaluable record of a carefully orchestrated sequence: as soon as the news of the new policies being propounded by the Beijing and Shanghai revolutionary groups was digested in Harbin, the local Party authorities moved swiftly against the "old ways." In its initial visible form, this was manifested in the destruction of the local Buddhist temples, the public defacement of Buddhist images and the burning of the sutras, and the public excoriation of the monks who had been tending the temples. But at the same time — and vividly shown here for the late August and early September period of 1966 — the attacks swung also against the leading Party officials in Harbin. Li unforgettably caught these men, each forced to carry a placard branding him for his crimes, compelled to stand on chairs the better to be jeered by the massive crowds of spectators, and mocked by being forced to wear elaborately elongated dunce caps. One of Li's most brilliant sequences shows the former governor of Heilongjiang having his hair slashed in jagged cuts by local self-appointed Red Guard leaders, an action providing vivid proof that these men and women no longer had the power to curb the revolution in their own communities. But — and this is important — these humiliations were encouraged and, to some extent, orchestrated by the newly appointed first secretary of the Heilongjiang Communist

Party committee, an outsider to the area without local ties named Pan Fusheng. He and several others kept their own power and were thus spared humiliation by offering up their previous fellow officials in the Party who had not had the foresight to prepare their own defensive positions.

In some of Li's early photographs of these upheavals, one can see the clearly displayed portraits of the Party leadership in Beijing; flanking Mao Zedong and Zhou Enlai one can recognize the familiar images of China's head of state Liu Shaoqi, and the national Party general secretary Deng Xiaoping. By the end of the year, however, both of these men had been dismissed and purged: Liu was to die shortly after, while Deng survived to lead China into a new direction after Mao's death.

The escalating violence and chaos can be seen in the images from the summer of 1967, when Li was able to capture the destruction of property and library volumes, and some of the human casualties of the vicious fighting that broke out between the various Red Guard groups. This was perhaps the peak of the violence in Harbin as elsewhere in China and led to Mao's realization that the destruction was now out of control. His solution was to order the army to play a determinant role in reestablishing order, albeit under an alleged structure of revolutionary Party solidarity, while the groups of marauding youth were to be disarmed and sent out to distant rural areas so that they could "learn from the peasants." These changes were not however made without further human loss: in April 1968, Li photographed seven men and one woman who were paraded through the streets and then shot kneeling in a neat row before a crowd of onlookers after their condemnation as criminals and counterrevolutionaries. In fact their fate seems to have sprung from the tangled local political situation in Harbin in which the army had allied itself with the so-called progressive workers in order to curb the local "anarchy" in the city. The public deaths of these eight people were therefore a public statement that "order" was henceforth to be maintained from the military center. What they had or had not done may well have been irrelevant.

After the start of 1969, the media, with the encouragement of Party authorities, tended to focus largely on the "positive" aspects of society that the Chinese government presented as proof that order had been restored. The glistening health of people busy with their constructive lives was one that fitted pleasantly enough into the period in which Mao's power to disrupt was on the wane, and reminds us that portentous changes were underway in China. It was at this time that the era of "ping-pong diplomacy" began and that, despite the ongoing Vietnam War, Mao and his advisers started responding to the United States' overtures that would bring President Richard Nixon to the halls of Beijing in early 1972. The massive rallies and the rows of corpses had now been transmuted, via Li's camera, to the staged loyalties of the "anti-Lin Biao and anti-Confucius" campaign of 1974, a curious intellectual venture that sought to show how reactionary impulses could spring from apparently revolutionary situations and how the need for strong authoritarian rule might therefore still be needed in Chinese society, as Mao himself, though aging and ill, could still replicate the roles of China's founding emperor more than two thousand years before.

Li began teaching photography in Beijing in the 1980s, but before beginning that new life he caught one more strange and eventful moment from his native Heilongjiang. The world had changed in China since the Cultural Revolution days, as least to this extent: that something approaching a minor capitalist movement was under way, as farmers were given more rights to till their lands under long-term family contracts, and some small pockets of local market freedom and spaces for individual entrepreneurs appeared in some cities. In this changing economic climate, with Mao dead and the remaining cultural revolutionary leaders themselves at last under arrest, a new genre of "exposure journalism" began to emerge, a journalism that bore a new kind of witness to the country's many problems. One of the most famous of these exposes dealt with a case in Heilongjiang, unearthed in 1978, in which a woman official named Wang Shouxin was able to corner the market in coal procurement and to build a small commercial empire out of connections, greed, coercion, and graft. It was a complicated case and took some time to unravel. But when the facts were in, Wang Shouxin was shot. For a last time, Li was able to catch an image of sad and lonely violence in the snows of Heilongjiang. Wang's death was intended by the authorities to be seen as exemplary punishment. But something about Li's photographs makes us wonder if things were quite that simple. Perhaps it is Wang Shouxin's face, peering back at us from the rear of the army truck taking her to the execution ground, her jaw dislocated by guards so that she can cry out no more with pleas or insults. Perhaps it is the calmness with which she kneels on the cold ground. But whatever it is, there is an ambiguity there that compels us to keep on asking questions about the meaning of what we think we are seeing. It is a fitting closure to Li Zhensheng's remarkable portrayal of terrible times.

Early dawn in the countryside
of Heilongjiang province.
21 December 1964

I..."IT IS RIGHT TO REBEL"

黑龙江日报

第4355期　1966年8月19日　星期五　夏历丙午年七月初四

毛泽东同志和林彪同志在天安门城楼上。　　新华社记者摄（传真照片）

我们的伟大领袖、伟大统帅、伟大舵手毛主席在天安门城楼上向群众挥手致意。

我们伟大的领袖、伟大的统帅、伟大的舵手毛主席万岁！

无产阶级文化大革命是共产主义运动和社会主义革命的伟大创举

毛主席同百万群众共庆文化大革命

毛主席和林彪周恩来等同志接见学生代表并检阅文化革命大军的游行队伍

毛主席说："这个运动规模很大，确实把群众发动起来了，对全国人民的思想革命化有很大的意义。"

林彪周恩来同志发表重要讲话，北京哈尔滨长沙南京等地革命师生也讲了话

新华社北京十八日电　我们的伟大领袖、伟大统帅、伟大舵手毛主席，今天同北京和来自全国各地的百万革命群众一起，在无产阶级革命的中心、在我们伟大祖国的首都、在雄伟的天安门广场，举行了庆祝无产阶级文化大革命的大会。

今天清晨五时许，太阳刚从东方地平线上射出万丈光芒，毛主席就来到了人群如海、红旗如林的天安门广场，会见了早已从四面八方汇集到这里的革命群众。毛主席身穿一套草绿色的布军装，主席的军帽上一颗红星闪闪发光。毛主席走过天安门前金水桥，一直走进群众的队伍当中，同周围的许多人紧紧握手，并且向全场革命群众招手致意。这时，广场上群情激动，人人双手举过头顶，向着毛主席跳跃着，欢呼着，许多人把手拿心都拍红了，许多人流下了激动的眼泪，他们欢喜地喊："毛主席来了！毛主席周我们中国来了！"广场上，万众欢声高呼："毛主席万岁！万岁！万万岁！"欢呼声一阵高过一阵，震荡着首都的天空。

我们伟大的领袖毛主席，在今天上午整整六个多小时中。一直和百万革命群众在一起。在检阅百万无产阶级文化革命大军的庆祝游行时，毛主席和林彪同志并肩地站在天安门上，看着浩浩荡荡的游行队伍，高兴地对林彪同志说："这个运动规模很大，确实把群众发动起来了，对全国人民的思想革命化有很大的意义。"

几百万系着红袖章的"红卫兵"们，英姿勃勃，象生龙活虎一样。在今天的大会上很引人注目。"红卫兵"是首都大中学生在无产阶级文化大革命运动中创建的革命群众组织，他们表示要一辈子当保卫毛主席、保卫党中央、保卫祖国的红色尖兵。在天安门城楼上，在天安门城楼前面东西的观礼台上，站满了"红卫兵"的代表。在天安门广场上，在广场两侧的东西长安街上，今天都由雄赳赳的"红卫兵"维持会场秩序。

在大会进行中，师大女附中一个"红卫兵"，登上天安门城楼给毛主席戴上了"红卫兵"的袖章。毛主席十分高兴地和她亲切握手。"红卫兵"，无限欢欣，有的一跃把跳。非常激动地说："毛主席是我们的统帅，我们是他的战士。""有的说："毛主席参加了我们的'红卫兵'，对我们是最大的支持和鼓励。毛主席给我们撑腰，我们什么也不怕。" **（下转第二版）**

革命小将"红卫兵"，千亲万焉，意气风发，他们正在这今天的，在无产阶级文化大革命中奋勇革命闯将。新华社记者摄（传真照片）

I.

The day after I was born, my father wrote my grandfather a letter asking him to name me. My grandfather was just a simple farmer in Shandong province, but he had studied for the county examinations during the Qing dynasty and was known as a very educated man for "ten *li* and eight villages around." In time, he would name all nineteen of his grandchildren, both boys and girls.

Consulting the Book of Changes, the *I-ching*, my grandfather determined that for me the most propitious name would be written with twenty-nine brush strokes. According to the family tree of names, *Zhen* was the generation's given name for boys; behind it, my grandfather added *Sheng*. Together these two characters were short for: "Like a soaring song your fame will touch the four corners of the world." Using this name, my grandfather then divined my fortune: I would not be a manual worker, it predicted. I would go to college, make money, and my renown would exceed even his. It would also be a life full of hardships — but I would survive; I would always find help when I needed it, and by the time I reached old age, I would no longer have any worries.

That was in the fall of 1940. The port city of Dalian in Liaoning province where my parents lived was occupied by the Japanese along with the rest of northeastern China — part of the puppet state Manchukuo — and there was little reason for optimism. My father was a cook on a steamship, a very good cook, who sometimes sailed to Hong Kong, Korea, Taiwan, even Singapore, but because of the fighting during the Second World War, there was a slowdown in shipping and he lost his job. Then, when I was three, my mother died, a few months after giving birth to my younger sister. Of her, I don't have a single trace of memory.

After my mother's death, to escape the tumult of the war my father decided to move the family back to his hometown, a small village in Rongcheng county in Shandong province, which was under the control of anti-Japanese forces, both Nationalists and Communists. There was also another reason. Like many men of his generation, my father had two wives. When he married my mother in Dalian he was still married to another woman in his hometown. He even had a son with her. After my mother died, his first wife wrote him a letter telling him to come back to the village and offering to take care of my sister and me.

Front page of the *Heilongjiang Daily*, 19 August 1966 reporting Mao Zedong's first review of the Red Guards from Tiananmen Gate in Beijing the previous day. Beneath the photographs of Mao and Marshal Lin Biao, the main headline reads, "Chairman Mao celebrates the Great Cultural Revolution with millions of people."

In September of 1944, when I turned four and my sister Shufang was less than a year old, we sailed off from Dalian. I remember that it was night and I couldn't see a thing. But in the morning, after we arrived at Weihai on the other side of Bo Hai harbor, we rode in the back of a horse cart to our village, fifty kilometers away. Along the way, every so often we saw Japanese planes flying very low in the sky, and frightened, leapt off the cart and hid in the fields by the road.

There were about three hundred people in the village in Rongcheng. We lived in a brick-and-stone peasant house with a dirt floor. No electricity, only gas lamps. No running water, only a village well two kilometers away — everyone together in one room: my sister and I, my father and his wife, and my half-brother, Zhenli, who was eight years older than me.

Li Zhensheng with his parents on the eve of his first birthday in Dalian, Liaoning province. 22 September 1941

Life in the countryside was tough. My father had to work in the fields. I was only seven or eight, but I remember helping him pick up the loose wheat during harvest, even pulling the plow. We used spades and did everything manually. Once I recall the two of us trying to push a one-wheel cart of manure up a slope. I had to walk in front, and no matter how hard I pulled, the cart wouldn't budge. When I looked at my father for instructions, he shouted: "Why did you turn around? Pull harder! Walk forward!" — because he really didn't know how to do it himself.

Having lost his job in the city and out of step with country life, my father grew agitated and was easily upset. He often quarreled with his wife. This was especially hard on their son Zhenli. Basically, his mother transferred all her love to my sister and me. She took us as her own children, and in turn from then on we always regarded her as our mother. She was particularly devoted to Shufang, who was very frail. A lot of people even told my father she wouldn't survive, but our new mother gave her all her love — if the hen laid an egg, she would cook it for her — and she got well.

As the Nationalists and the Communists fought over the province, some joined Chiang Kai-shek's forces, and some joined Mao Zedong. Zhenli enlisted in Mao's Revolutionary Army. He was only sixteen but lied about his age to sign up. If he joined the army he could support himself, be independent; but my father's quarreling, my mother shifting her love, these, I think, were the real reasons he left — because he felt neglected. I've carried guilt about this all my life. More than fifty years have passed, and I still cannot say my brother's name without feeling tears come to my eyes.

Zhenli was with Mao's People's Liberation Army when he was killed in September 1949, in a place called Mouping. It was a few weeks before the end of the civil war. He was seventeen. One day a village cadre came to our house, and afterward my mother burst into tears. Then they put up a wooden sign on the door, saying: "Glorious Family of Martyr." I was only nine, but I was beginning to understand what was going on around me. One thing I clearly remember is that afterward, during the Spring Festival, the Chinese New Year, the village cadres would lead a group of people to our house, all banging drums and gongs, and hang a red lantern in front. Across the street, another family who had sent their son to join Chiang Kai-shek's army was given a black one. The area had since been liberated by Chairman Mao's army, so that was done just to humiliate them.

My family was considered a revolutionary family — my father even joined the Party — but I don't think my parents really cared about politics. They were at the bottom of society, just trying to make a living.

Because I had to help with the farming, I didn't go to elementary school until I was ten. By then the new China had been founded, in October 1949. "Born in the old society but grown up under the Red Flag" — a familiar way of referring to my generation — I was among the first "Chinese Young Pioneers," the first group to wear the red scarf. My mother cut me one from a piece of red cloth, but I remember it came out too short and was always very awkward to wear. We were told by our teacher that the scarf represented a corner of the red flag of revolution, dyed bright with the fresh blood of the revolutionary martyrs. Like my brother's, I thought.

After the war, my father decided to return to Dalian alone. He didn't go back to the ship, but instead got a job as a cook in the hospice of the Seaman's Trade Union. He was intent on my becoming a *dragon*, a success. And since the only path to becoming a dragon was education, and the better schools were in the city, I followed him two years later. He was living in a dormitory for singles and had a roommate, so when I first arrived I stayed with my maternal grandmother. But every Sunday my father took me to a movie, then to sleep over at his dorm. There were about a dozen movie houses in Dalian. They didn't show American films, only films from the Soviet Union and other socialist Eastern European countries like Poland and Czechoslovakia. At that time, relations between China and the Soviet Union were very good. There was a major Soviet naval base in the city. All the Young Pioneers joined the Sino-Soviet Friendship Society, and we each received a certificate and a small pin with a double profile of Mao Zedong and Joseph Stalin. I remember that there was a slogan: "The Soviet Union today is China tomorrow."

Maybe it's because I was from the countryside, but I had such a passion for the movies I even saved my ticket stubs. To earn money for the price of admission I collected empty aluminum toothpaste tubes. I could sell them for three cents each, and for a while I even brushed my teeth with heapings of paste, trying to finish the tube quicker — that is, until my grandmother realized what I was doing and got very upset. But I had another trick. At that time, to lure people into the theater they usually had

Family picture taken by Li (fifth from right) with his 4.5 x 6 camera set on a self-timer. Li's grandfather Li Xingcun is seated in the center. Lidao commune, Rongcheng county, Shandong province. 18 February 1958

loudspeakers in front broadcasting what was going on inside. So when I couldn't afford a ticket, I just stood in front of theater and *listened* to the movie, trying to imagine the image of the film. I even took notes. Then, when the film was over, I compared them to what my friends in the audience had really seen.

I was very keen on drawing, so when I was in middle school I studied painting three nights a week at the Dalian Popular Fine Arts Center. One day a representative from a textile mill saw one of my drawings in a student exhibit and decided to use some of my illustrations for floral patterns on a fabric. Later, other drawings of mine were used too. One even became a design on a washbasin. I felt a real sense of achievement when I saw *that*! I thought, "This is designed by me" — and I made up my mind to become a painter.

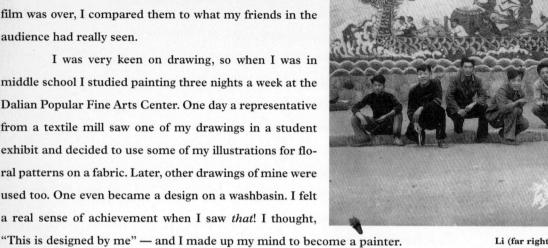

Li (far right) with classmates during the Great Leap Forward movement in front of the anti-imperialist mural they painted near their school in Dalian. 1 October 1958

When the Great Leap Forward began in 1958, it was truly exciting. In fifteen years, we were told, we would catch up with, even surpass, the living standards of Britain and the United States! The whole country was mobilized. Everyone collected scrap metal to boost the country's steel production, and fiery makeshift furnaces melted it down all over town.

Because I could draw well, I was asked to be part of a team instructed to create a big mural. We painted a fifteen-foot-long dragon boat blazing forward through the waves. On it, Chinese workers and peasants with drums and gongs were celebrating their victory over America and Britain, represented by two smaller boats lagging behind, their sailors gazing at the dragon boat in despair. I really felt that I was contributing something to society.

About this time, our middle-school physics teacher set up a photography club. Because he knew I was good at painting, he asked me to become the group leader. The school owned a Czechoslovakian-made 120 Brownie-type camera, so everybody used that. That's how I started taking pictures. My interest in photography grew when I saw an exhibition of fine-art photography from the Soviet Union, and I began collecting postcards sent back from the 1956 World Youth Festival in Moscow, mostly photographs of beautiful scenic landscapes. The movie stills around the film posters outside the theaters also made a deep impression on me, since I looked at them for long periods while listening to the movies inside.

In those days my father gave me eight *yuan* every month — the equivalent of about one dollar today. I spent most of it on food, but with the bit I was able to save I took up stamp collecting. Over time, I assembled a collection from many countries, and I had themes: stamps of writers, poets, painters, famous paintings — always something to do with fine arts or culture. All the stamp collectors gathered on a particular corner near the Victory Bridge Post Office, the largest one in the city. One day I met a middle-aged man there who had just started collecting. He didn't have any of the stamps I did and wanted mine so badly he offered to swap me a Japanese 120 camera for two hundred of them. So the first camera I had was by trading my stamps.

Owning a camera was a real luxury then, and that a middle-school student had one was really incredible. Only, I couldn't afford to buy any film. A roll cost one *yuan*, an eighth of my monthly living allowance. My classmates, though, all knew I had a camera and often asked me to take pictures of them. They provided the film — sometimes pooling their money to buy a roll — and, as compensation, let me use one of the sixteen frames for myself. When I took these pictures for them I was always so meticulous about composition and lighting that I usually couldn't finish a roll in one day, in a single setting. So I would just go out and whenever I found something interesting, make my shot.

At that time I planned to go to a fine-arts school. I never even considered studying cinematography because there was only one film school in China and it was in Beijing. But during the Great Leap Forward it was decided that every province had to have a film studio, and needing trained people to work in them, the Ministry of Culture planned to open two new film schools, one in Shanghai and another in Changchun.

The Changchun Film School was in the capital of the neighboring province Jilin, and the entrance examination was held in four different cities in northeastern China, including Dalian. Even though I was only in my first year of high school, my principal encouraged me to sit in on the exam. At first I didn't think I could do it, but for a week I pored through stacks of books trying to learn everything related to cinema, whether it was chemistry or physics or fine arts, and decided to take the test.

Right: Li photographed by his classmate Zheng Lianyi at the entrance of the Changchun Film School during his second year in Changchun, Jilin province. 25 December 1961. Far right: Premier Zhou Enlai (far right) during an impromptu inspection of the Changchun Film School. 22 August 1962

As it happened, the exam was held in the same place where I had taken my painting classes. There were 160 candidates for one vacancy in the cinematography department, and everyone sat together in one big room. On the blackboard were questions: "Have you read the works of Konstantin Stanislavsky? What are his main ideas?" One young man raised his hand. "Who is Stanislavsky?" he asked. In the entire group, nobody knew. "A Soviet dramatist," I called out. Everyone turned to look at me in surprise. "Well, what are his works?" the teacher asked. I had once leafed through a book of his in the library, and from memory I said, *An Actor Prepares*. Impressed, the teacher said, "That's good enough. There's no need to go further."

Of course, a week of studying can't cover much. But what the cinematography department was really looking for in a candidate was the ability to draw well. They asked us to make sketches: a foot, a face, geometrical forms — and the three years of night classes I had spent studying painting really paid off. The school had five departments, including directing, scriptwriting, and performing, and two — cinematography and writing — wanted to have me. I chose cinematography.

Despite the people's enthusiasm, the Great Leap Forward was a disaster, and from 1960 to 1962 China was devastated by the great famine. More than twenty million people are believed to have died. Food was scarce throughout the country, and I suffered from malnutrition like everyone else, but what really saved me at this time was my girlfriend, Sun Peikui. She was a student in the performing department, studying to become an actress. Our school was on the grounds of the Changchun Film Studio,

Li's first love, Sun Peikui, in front of a billboard advertising a Chinese opera–based film entitled *Lychee Mirror* in Harbin, Heilongjiang province. 26 August 1966

and when our paths crossed in the yard, she would furtively slip me extra ration coupons she had somehow managed to save up.

Peikui was my first true love. In the summer of 1962 I even took her to Dalian to meet my father. One day while we were there, we went to the beach, and I discovered that she didn't know how to swim. I tried to teach her, but she wouldn't allow me to touch her. So instead we had to get her an inner tube to keep her afloat.

During the Great Leap Forward they upsized everything. Now, with the famine, the Party leadership realized they had to *downsize*. The new film studios were to be shut down. They decided to close my school the following year. The course work was supposed to have lasted three years, followed by a film project in the fourth. Instead

Marchers in Harbin during the National Day parade carry large wooden characters that read, "Long live the People's Republic of China," and banners with the profiles of Marx, Engels, Lenin, and Stalin followed by one of Mao Zedong. The Russian Orthodox cathedral of St. Sophia is visible in the background.
1 October 1963

they now instructed all cinematography students to convert to photojournalism.

As class monitor I called a meeting. My classmates and I were extremely upset over the decision to abolish the cinematography department. In the back of our classroom we had a banner with the slogan, "We dedicate our youth to the film enterprise of the Party"; now we were told we would never make films.

At that time the director of the National Film Bureau arranged a visit to the Changchun Film Studio. We decided that three of us, including myself, should go speak with him. When the school authorities found out, they told us not to do it. The other two classmates were older than me. One had been a doctor, the other a teacher. They'd gone through the anti-rightist campaign against intellectuals in 1957, and they knew we wouldn't get anywhere and would just end up in trouble. So at the last minute they begged off. The teacher suddenly had an appointment; the doctor had to go home. But I didn't know any of this and went ahead.

The director was actually quite open. When he went back to Beijing he told the Xinhua News Agency that we all had solid cinematography training and would make excellent photojournalists. The agency selected five of us, including me. But because I hadn't "listened to the Party" and had gone over the heads of the school authorities, the principal of my school decided not to let me go.

Those selected studied English at a foreign-language institute, and the person who replaced me eventually ended up becoming the correspondent for the Xinhua News Agency in Washington, DC — so I missed a once-in-a-lifetime opportunity. Instead I was assigned to work at the Information Research Institute of the Heilongjiang Science and Technology Commission, making microfiche of foreign scientific and technical documents. The job was in Harbin, capital of the far-flung province of Heilongjiang, which bordered the Soviet Union.

I took the train there. The information section chief who met me at the commission explained that there were a lot of job benefits. For example, you could study a foreign language, travel. But he also told me that because the job dealt with classified material, once you worked there you could never transfer out. I could see my whole life projected in front of me. I'll be bored to death, I thought, and I immediately went to the personnel section and told them the job didn't accord with the basic principles of my training. Had Vice-Premier and Foreign Minister Marshal Chen Yi not stated that university graduates should make full use of what they learned in college? Actually, the head of personnel agreed with me. My files were sent back to the Bureau of Education, and I was told, "If you want, look for a job by yourself."

So forty years ago I set out looking for a job on my own, which was very unusual in China. First, I applied for a position at the Agricultural Exhibition Hall. They were looking for someone to take pictures for exhibits related to farming, and offered me a job on the spot. With one bird in hand, when I left the hall I quietly asked for directions to the municipal newspaper, the *Harbin Daily*. I took a bus there. They wanted me too, and I thought to myself, "I should aim higher."

The *Heilongjiang Daily* was the largest news-paper in the province, with a circulation of about 270,000. Its headquarters, a city landmark, sat on the top of a hill up the slope from the municipal paper. No sooner had I walked out the door of the city paper than I started making my way there. I remember passing a very big department store with attractive window displays — but I was in no mood to linger.

Li, his father, his stepmother, and his sister (right to left), upon Li's return to his hometown for the Spring Festival marking the Chinese New Year (photographed with a self-timer). Lidao commune, 28 January 1965

When I arrived at the paper at the top of the hill, I was interviewed by the head of personnel. My file was still with the Bureau of Education, and she wanted to know if there was anything against me in it. I told her the story about how I had bypassed the authorities at the film school to speak with the director of the National Film Bureau, but she didn't see anything much wrong with that. She went upstairs and returned with an older man. He merely asked me to walk back and forth in front of him for a while and then to turn around so he could have a good look at me. Then he left the room.

The man turned out to be the editor in chief, Zhao Yang. Why was I asked to walk around the room? Because, I found out after I was hired, at that time the paper had four photographers. One was as tall and skinny as a lamppost, one was fat and round like a ball, and the other two were so short they were almost midgets. This irritated Zhao, who felt that the *Heilongjiang Daily*, as a newspaper that covered the entire province as well as visits by foreign guests, needed to have at least one presentable photographer. Apparently having met his criteria, I started at the *Heilongjiang Daily* in August 1963.

That evening I wrote in my diary, "I am not going to die in Heilongjiang province."

For my first two months at the paper I was assigned to help a police precinct in Harbin collect data for a household registration survey — but hardly had I started, it seemed, before I was sent down to the countryside. This was during the Socialist Education Movement when thousands of young people were dispatched to rural areas to share the hardship of the peasants and to stir up revolutionary fervor. If you hadn't been a soldier, a worker, or a peasant, you needed to go. And I was among the first participants.

In October 1964 I arrived at a commune in Acheng county, about fifty kilometers southeast of Harbin. Coming from the city, I found the experience truly eye-opening. The county was very backward and life there entirely different. Holding bayonets, we had to train with the militia in the morning. Then we visited the homes of poor peasants and listened to them recall their sufferings in the old China. The peasants didn't trust us. It didn't matter that we helped them till the fields and harvest, paid for the meals we shared with them, even lived under the same roof. They knew we would leave eventually, and everything would be just as it was.

Along with four other young men from the city, I was assigned to live with a poor peasant in branch number four of the Donghuan production brigade. We slept on a *kang*, a brick bed heated from below. There were two in the room, and the warmer one facing south was reserved for the owner of the house. We five young men from the city slept together on the other *kang*, which was less than three meters wide. At meals, months would go by without meat; if there were one or two drops of cooking oil, the food tasted delicious.

Sometimes, when we just couldn't stand the harsh conditions anymore, my friends and I would head off to the town of Acheng, the county center, and buy something to eat, maybe even go to a restaurant. We would make sure not to order anything too expensive, just a couple of dishes, a few bottles of beer maybe. But the authorities found out about it anyway, just as they found out about my diary and my love letters to Peikui, and in the end we all had to make a self-criticism.

Photograph of Li (far left) with members of his work team dining at a small restaurant in Acheng, Heilongjiang province, during the Socialist Education Movement — an extravagance for which they were subsequently reprimanded (photographed with a self-timer). 25 April 1965

In front of all forty team members of branch number four, I criticized myself for having "bourgeois thoughts" and afterward listened attentively as the team members gave exaggerated speeches analyzing my errors. To show my acceptance of their critisism and my eagerness to reform, I even took notes. At the conclusion of the meeting, I promised to "study Chairman Mao's works harder" and to "follow the Party's instructions forever."

Mine were not serious "class-enemy" offenses, so there was no slogan shouting or fist waving. But the work team leaders reported back to *Heilongjiang Daily* that I had broken the "three-together" rule: eating, living, and

Li holding his Russian-made Kiev 35 mm camera and a German 6 x 6 Rolleiflex in Ashihe commune, Acheng county (photograph by Liu Guoqi). 12 May 1965

working with the peasants. Because of this — and because I was later asked to spend several months taking photographs for an exhibition on the Socialist Education Movement — when my year in the countryside was up, the authorities at the newspaper thought I hadn't had enough of a chance to be reeducated. That's why, while most returned, I was sent to another commune in Bayan county, about sixty kilometers northeast of Harbin, for an additional term.

I came back in March 1966. The Cultural Revolution broke out in May.

1964–1966

In 1964, the first tremors of the decade-long cataclysm known as the Cultural Revolution began to shake the Chinese countryside. The Socialist Education Movement, launched by Mao Zedong the previous year, started as a campaign against corruption and ideological backsliding. In reality, it was a dress rehearsal for the great chaos to come, a prelude to the anarchy and class struggle the Chairman would unleash to deepen the communist revolution, purge all enemies, and establish himself once and for all as the sole and infallible ruler of China.

Five years earlier, Mao had retired to the political sidelines. His Great Leap Forward, which sought to boost grain and steel production and collect the entire nation into a vast network of "people's communes," had sparked one of the most colossal human tragedies in modern history: a famine that would kill over twenty million people. Stung by the movement's failure and the ensuing criticism of his policies, Mao left the rebuilding of the country largely to the new head of state, President Liu Shaoqi. By 1965, under a variety of liberalizing reforms that saw the Chairman's prestige wane and power in the communes decentralized, China had recovered — but at a cost Mao considered personally and ideologically treacherous.

Now the seventy-year-old former guerrilla hero whose peasant revolution had given birth to the People's Republic of China set out one last time to unleash the power of the masses. Goaded by Mao's cry to "nip the counterrevolution in the bud!" millions of "educated youth" — primarily high-school graduates from the cities — flooded rural areas to "learn from the peasants." Meanwhile droves of urban government and Party cadres — work teams — arrived at country communes for yearlong stays to propagate socialist values. Beginning with the "four cleanups" of accounting procedures, granary supplies, property accumulation, and the payment-compensation system of work points, these teams, together with local commune leaders, organized mass rallies and public criticisms against landlords, rich peasants, counterrevolutionaries, and other supposed bad characters — the "four elements." In the years preceding the official outbreak of the Great Proletarian Cultural Revolution in 1966, these events grew in both size and frequency, gradually evolving into an epic witch-hunt for all class enemies.

Ashihe commune, Acheng county, Heilongjiang province, 20 November 1964

During the Socialist Education
Movement, a work-team leader
instructs peasants on the "four
cleanups" and how to rid the
countryside of anti-Party elements.

A peasant criticized as a class enemy is forced to bow in the traditional acknowledgment of guilt (below). Encouraged to make personal accusations against the denounced, a young woman attacks fellow peasant Zhang Diange for "unreasonably" pressuring her father to repay a debt on time (opposite).

Liaodian and Ashihe communes, Acheng county, 27 February–25 March 1965

Under a banner that reads
"Struggle against the enemies rally,"
Zhang Diange is denounced as a
rich peasant by members of the
Nansheng production brigade
and made to bow his head for hours.

Ashihe commune, Acheng county, 25 March 1965

Ashihe commune, Acheng county, 27–28 March 1965

The formation of the people's communes represents one of the most radical social experiments in modern history. A vast program to organize the country's six hundred million inhabitants into over twenty thousand self-sufficient work camps, it sought to replace China's traditional family structure and strong filial tradition with a militaristic regimentation in which members would work together and eat in communal canteens, sublimating their individual energies to the good of the collective.

Over time, power in the communes devolved to smaller multi-village units called production brigades. These brigades, with a leadership elected from a slate of handpicked Party candidates, became the dominant force in people's lives, controlling work assignments and militia duties. Largely engaged in farming, brigade members typically spent their days working the land with only their bare hands and draft animals, and their evenings studying the writings of Chairman Mao.

Ashihe commune, Acheng county, 16–18 April 1965

Alternating work in the fields with military exercises, production brigade members are trained in militia techniques (opposite). After work, they spend hours studying Mao's works and reading Party-controlled newspapers such as the *China Youth Daily*, including this one with the headline "Vietnamese troops shoot down twelve American planes for a total of over one hundred in seven months" (above).

Ashihe commune, Acheng county, 20 April 1965

Working conditions in the arid
province of Heilongjiang were
extremely rudimentary, as peasants
depended mainly on draft animals
and their own physical labor to sow
millet, one the region's main crops.

With a banner proclaiming "It's a glorious road to the countryside," leaders and local residents of the town of Acheng send off a group of "educated youth" to participate in the Socialist Education Movement (below). Members of the Donghuan production brigade of Ashihe commune announce the founding of the "Poor and Lower-Middle Peasant Association" to represent their interests on a county-wide basis (opposite).

Acheng county, 28–29 April 1965

At the heart of the Socialist Education Movement, forerunner to the Cultural Revolution, was a phenomenon to have enormous influence in the years to come: the "struggle sessions." During these events, men and women condemned as one of the "four elements" were publicly criticized by friends and neighbors, even family members, while forced to bow their head in a display of guilt. These public spectacles and their key weapon — humiliation — would provide a blueprint for activity during the revolution to come.

Organized by work teams and commune authorities, struggle sessions, lasting hours, took place in lieu of work, with attendance by all commune members mandatory. Frequently what transpired was a freewheeling settling of scores as peasants, encouraged to inform against one another, manufactured accusations of often specious content under the guise of ideological purity. For the condemned, such as those in China's northeastern province of Heilongjiang, criticism typically resulted in consignment to hard labor, including breaking up frozen earth or carrying buckets of human waste. Those accused of being landlords or rich peasants additionally faced the confiscation of their property. In the years before the Cultural Revolution's start, these seized "mansions" — often rudimentary dwellings — were transformed into museums of bourgeois decadence throughout China and visited by millions.

Ashihe commune, Acheng county, 12 May 1965

A local peasant activist leads the crowd in chanting slogans during a "fight against the enemies" rally before rich peasants and other anti-Party elements are brought forth to be criticized.

Ashihe commune, Acheng county, 12 May 1965

Denounced as a rich peasant,
Deng Guoxing bows before a sea
of accusers during a three-hour-
long "struggle session."

Yuan Fengxiang (below) is
denounced as a rich peasant by
a local woman, Chen Xiuhua
(opposite).

Ashihe commune, Acheng county, 12 May 1965

Ashihe commune, Acheng county, 12 May 1965

Yuan Fengxiang and Deng Guoxing
(opposite, left and right) are made
to stand with their heads bowed
while being sentenced to two years
of hard labor. The local and county
leaders who determined the sentence engage in casual banter as
the accused are led away (above).

Ashihe commune, Acheng county, 13 May 1965

Following his denunciation, Yuan Fengxiang's property is transformed into a class-education exhibition center. Peasants from all over the county come to visit the "landlord mansion" (opposite), where the family's personal belongings — red and green house lights, a Swiss watch, a deerskin jacket, a silk dress and stockings, a leather jacket lined with lamb's wool, and money boxes, among other items — are displayed as evidence of their bourgeois status (above).

Accused peasants are kept under guard by local militia as they wait to be denounced at a mass rally as one of the "four elements" — landlords, rich peasants, counter-revolutionaries, or "bad characters" — as indicated by the sign.

Liaodian commune, Acheng county, 13 May 1965

Organized in production brigades, peasants are assigned back-breaking farmwork such as constructing pigsties (below) and tilling fields (opposite).

Liaodian commune, Acheng county, 14–16 May 1965

Residents of the town of Acheng
gather at a mass rally to denounce
Hang Jingshan as a "bad character"
and a "speculator" — someone
involved in illegal commerce.
He is arrested by the local police
after publicly admitting his "crime"
(far right).

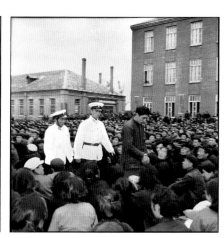

A major international power by 1964, the People's Republic of China was also one of the world's most isolated countries. It was not recognized by the United Nations, where its seat was held by Chiang Kai-shek's Taiwan, and was at odds with both the great superpowers: the United States, its ideological enemy, and supporter of Chiang; and the Soviet Union, once its greatest ally but, since Nikita Khrushchev's 1959 repudiation of Mao's former ally Joseph Stalin, its greatest threat. Faced with increased Soviet military activity on its northern border and alarmed by the U.S. presence in Vietnam to the south, Mao's response was to assemble a vast people's militia that would soon claim ten million members.

Set within the bitterly cold region at the foot of the Russian steppes on China's northern border, the province of Heilongjiang had long been defined by its proximity to the U.S.S.R. Its major cities were spurs of the Russian railways, and during the 1950s, when Sino-Soviet relations were at their peak and "learn from the Soviet Union" a national motto, the province had been the flagship of Sino-Soviet friendship. As the rift between the two nations deepened in the following decade, Heilongjiang's Wusuli river became the scene of sporadic border skirmishes, and commune militias trained in the province's forests and fields, the nation's first line of defense against the "revisionist" enemy.

Acheng county, 30 May–27 June 1965

As part of the national defense against "Imperialism abroad and revisionists at home," schoolchildren of the "Little Red Militia" (opposite top) and workers from an electrical-component factory participate in militia drills (opposite bottom and below).

Acheng, Acheng county, 1 July 1965

In a middle-school meeting room,
new members of the Communist
Party take the oath in front of a
bust of Mao and the hammer and
sickle of the communist flag.

Acheng county, 30 June–2 July 1965

In the early 1960s, China experienced the full-scale growth of the propaganda machine that would indelibly shape the Cultural Revolution. Much of the new cultural production had one purpose: to elevate Mao. In 1963 Lei Feng, a foot soldier who had lived an unremarkable life, became a model of moral rectitude when his diary of blind devotion to Mao was "discovered" bearing the claim "It is glorious to be a nameless hero." By 1965, the idea of model citizens had extended to all fields: model soldiers, model peasants, and model workers in every vocation.

The elevation of propaganda as a primary tool for revolution had two main champions: Defense Minister Lin Biao, who made Lei Feng's diary required reading for all army members and produced the bible of the coming revolution, *Quotations of Chairman Mao —* the Little Red Book; and Mao's third wife, Jiang Qing, a former Shanghai B-movie actress who in 1965 provided the movement's opening wedge by assaulting the historical drama *The Dismissal of Hairui from Office*. Encompassing newspapers, films, song, dance, poetry, and opera, culture now became both a field of suspicion and a tool with which to wage revolution.

"Model" citizens chosen to set an example for others included Wang Shuangyin, composer of the famous revolutionary song "Rely on the Helmsman While Sailing the Seas" (opposite), and revolutionary hero Song Ranhao, who lost an arm in the Korean War, here showing off his skills and his faithful study of Mao's writings despite his injury (right).

Acheng, Acheng county, 12 July 1965

次贫下中农代表大会

高举毛泽东思想红旗，巩固社会
伟大成果，把社会主义革命进行到底

At the end of a one-day conference, the newly elected leaders of the county's Poor and Lower-Middle Peasants Association gather on the stage of the local theater. Banners encourage the attendees to "learn from Da Zhai [a model production brigade], to emulate Heilongjiang's model commune Dai Ping, and to work hard."

In the auditorium of the provincial capital's North Plaza Hotel, dancers from the Heilongjiang Song and Dance Company perform *Militia Women*, a piece about women training to join the fight against reactionaries and imperialists.

Harbin, Heilongjiang province, 25 April 1966

黑龙江日报

第4365期 1966年8月29日 星期一 夏历丙午年七月十四

这次无产阶级文化大革命，最高司令是我们毛主席。毛主席是统帅。我们在伟大统帅的指挥下，好好地听我们统帅——毛主席的话，文化大革命一定能顺利发展，一定能取得伟大胜利！

林彪

伟大的领袖伟大的統帅伟大的舵手毛主席万岁！

我们伟大的革命导师毛主席，日日夜夜为国际国内的大事操心。毛主席呼毛主席，我们一定听您的话，关心国家的大事，关心世界革命的大事，敢想、敢干、敢革命，用我们的双手，创造一个崭新的新世界！　　　新华社记者摄

毛主席的伟大号召越来越广泛地成为全国红卫兵的实际行动

学习解放军用毛泽东思想指导一切行动
把横扫"四旧"的斗争风暴推向新的高峰

据新华社北京二十八日电 我们的伟大领袖毛主席关于全国人民都学习解放军的伟大号召，正在越来越广泛地成为全国各地红卫兵和革命青少年的实际行动。各地红卫兵们纷纷表示，他们一定要象解放军那样，努力学习毛泽东思想，坚决贯彻毛泽东思想，积极宣传毛泽东思想，勇做坚决捍卫毛泽东思想领导自己的一切行动，敢于革命、善于革命，把横扫"四旧"的斗争风暴推向新的高峰，把无产阶级文化大革命进行到底。

广大红卫兵和革命的青少年，不愧为最坚决地响应毛主席的号召、最认真地向解放军学习的好榜样。他们不仅从小立志要当一名光荣的解放军战士，而且是无产阶级文化大革命冲锋陷阵，表现了最勇敢最坚决的敢于斗争、敢于革命的战斗精神。今天，《人民日报》的社论"向我们的榜样解放军学习"发表以后，首都和全国各地红卫兵和革命少年更是风风火火动，设千就干。一面认真学习《人民日报》社论，一面认真总结前一段开展无产阶级文化大革命的经验，制定新的行动注意；有的学习了解放军的三大纪律八项注意，学习了党和国家的有关政策，决心要象解放军那样成为执行群众纪律、执行党和国家政策的模范，把红卫兵建设成为具有高度组织性纪律性的革命青少年队伍。有的再一次学习了毛主席有关的指示，决心要让十六条和毛主席的指示办事，做毛主席的好战士，北京市东方红中学（原第二十八中）的那分红卫兵学习了这篇社论后，以解放军为榜样，重新修改、补充了原订的红卫兵九条纪律。他们特别强调要象解放军那样，全心全意为人民服务，永远做人民的勤务员，坚决执行三大纪律八项注意。

首都广大革命青少年怀着极大的革命热情，纷纷学习和宣传《人民日报》社论，认为这是对革命青少年成长的最大关怀，是对革命青少年的最大信任，是对解放军的最大信任，北京戏剧学院的红卫兵们说：解放军同绝的人斗争最坚决，对群众最热爱，学习解放军，就要学习他们一切资产阶级、修正主义，同时又善于团结、热爱人民群众。北京二中的红卫兵不久前就发出了充满革命豪情的向旧世界的宣战书，他们在斗争中经常对照解放军总政工部的要求，提高自己。他们认为，只有象解放军那样坚决地按照毛主席的指示和党的政策办事，才能真无不紧，战无不胜，东方红四中的许多红卫兵说，读毛主席的书，听毛主席的话，照毛主席的指示办事，做毛主席的好战士，北京市东方红中学（原第二十八中）的那分红卫兵学习了这篇社论后，以解放军为榜样，重新修改、补充了原订的红卫兵九条纪律。他们特别强调要象解放军那样，全心全意为人民服务，永远做人民的勤务员，坚决执行三大纪律八项注意。

上海许多大中学校的革命学生今天都认真讨论了《人民日报》的社论，他们决心要最坚决最热烈地响应毛主席的伟大号召，为解放军学习，做毛主席的好战士。上海戏剧学院的藏象学生，在文化大革命中誓对毛、学了毛主席那深厚的阶级感情，做毛主席坚持贯彻毛主席思想，执行十六条，今天他们在座谈《人民日报》社论时说，我们坚决向解放军那样，坚决地执行三大纪律八项注意，爱护群众，保卫人民利益，保卫国家财产。交通大学一名红卫兵说，毛主席亲自制定的十六条是我们行动的指南。

我们一定要象解放军那样最坚决地执行毛主席的指示，在文化大革命中坚决地执行十六条办事。我们要坚持文斗，不用武斗。

开封市许多红卫兵紧跟着十六条和《毛主席语录》，走到哪里宣传到哪里，看到反映"四旧"的名称就积极建议改革，同时认真拥护文物、古迹，红卫兵们来到"罗王合公园"向职工提出四项建议，把园名改为开封红卫公园，在门口树立毛主席巨幅画像，园内墙上写上毛主席语录，在文物、古碑旁加上批判说明。公园职工热烈欢迎、红卫兵们这样做的热烈拥护。沈阳市今天有数以千计的红卫兵传队走到街头连续宣传讲毛泽东思想。沈阳红卫兵们说：我们要宣传毛主席的话，毛主席怎么说，凡是符合毛泽东思想，符合十六条精神的，就是上刀山下火海，我们也坚决拥护，凡是违反毛泽东思想、违反十六条的，我们一定坚决反对。贵阳市女子中学的毛泽东思想活学活用毛主席著作小组，学习解放军，重温老英雄毛主席，学习解放军，重温老英雄，罗盛教、欧阳海、刘英俊的英雄事迹，要把宣传毛泽东思想当成终身的任务，永远做一个忠于毛泽东思想的红色宣传员。

II.

On 16 May 1966, the Chinese Communist Party Central Committee issued a document — the May 16 Notice — announcing the start of the Great Proletarian Cultural Revolution.

Everywhere people were genuinely excited. Their enthusiasm was real. They believed in Mao. They thought he was trying to prevent China from "changing its color," that we were all marching forward toward prosperity and a powerful state. When Mao said, "destroy the old and establish the new," everyone felt the same — that it was a *right* movement.

At the beginning of the Cultural Revolution I was very excited, too. Like hundreds of millions of people in China, I believed in Mao. He was the leader with the "great strategic thinking against imperialism and revisionism." He said we were going to have revolutions like this every seven or eight years, so young men like me were thinking that we were lucky, we were only in our twenties and would have the chance to experience several of them during our lifetimes. Mao once wrote that even though there are a lot of Marxist teachings, in the final analysis there is only one sentence that matters: "It is right to rebel." That summer, people took him at his word. Many students didn't return home during the vacation. Instead they stayed on campus to be part of the revolution. That was the summer of the Red Guard.

The Red Guards were part of a grassroots movement that basically sought to overthrow all authority. They sprang up first at a middle school in Beijing, then swept through the high schools and universities, quickly joined by thousands of other groups known as "rebels." Unlike the Young Pioneers or the Communist Youth League, none of them were under provincial control, and it was through them that Mao and the Central Committee would carry out the revolution.

Mao sat out the early turmoil of the Cultural Revolution in Hangzhou, near Shanghai. But after President Liu Shaoqi, his would-be successor, sent work teams to the universities to bring the movement under control, the Chairman returned to Beijing and decisively threw his weight behind the Red Guards — and against Liu. On 5 August 1966, Mao issued what he referred to as "my own big character poster." It said, "Bombard the Headquarters." The poster, an indirect accusation of Liu Shaoqi, pointed toward a "bourgeois headquarters" in the Central Committee of the Party. Thirteen days later, Mao appeared before a million Red Guards from a podium atop Tiananmen Gate and put on a Red Guard armband, giving the movement his symbolic blessing.

After that, it was like a small flame bursting into a big fire. In Harbin, as in cities all over China, great rallies and demonstrations took place. Sports fields and stadiums filled with enormous crowds, hundreds of thousands of people, making a noise

Front page of the *Heilongjiang Daily*, 29 August 1966. The vertical headline lists the "three greats": "Long life to Chairman Mao, Great Leader, Great Commander in Chief, Great Helmsman." The photo caption from the Xinhua news agency reads, "Our great revolutionary teacher Chairman Mao concerns himself with national and international affairs day and night."

so loud I could hear it all the way in my office at the newspaper.

Within a week, the city's rebel groups went on a rampage. First they attacked Saint Nicholas, the venerable wooden Russian Orthodox Cathedral, tearing it down with their bare hands. The next day they sacked the Buddhist Jile Temple. Thirty-seven years later I still cannot understand why they did what they did — why they smashed all the statues and burned the sacred books. They even made the monks hold up a banner that said, "To hell with the Buddhist scriptures. They are full of dog farts."

That was one of the most remarkable events of the summer, and naturally several photographers were there, including a senior photographer

This image of the Saint Nicholas Russian Orthodox church under assault by Harbin's Red Guards in the summer of 1966 was created by Li using two overlapping photographs to give the full vertical view (see original photographs on p. 94).

for the *Northeastern Forestry Journal*. Wanting to get a picture of the monks with their heads bowed, he told them to drop the banner. He even tried to tear it out of their hands. But I asked the monks to hold on to it — and since as a film student I knew that nothing was more expressive than the face, I asked them to lift their heads and look toward the camera. Afterward, they put the banner down and assumed the standard heads-bowed position, and the photographer from the *Forestry Journal* made his picture.

Two days later, tens of thousands of people in Harbin gathered in the People's Stadium — freshly renamed "Red Guard Square" — for a rally. The event was very well organized. Banners with slogans were set up, flags were raised, and after being seated, everyone chanted the "four greats" — "Long live our great teacher, our great leader, our great commander in chief, our great helmsman" — and sang revolutionary songs like "Rely on the Helmsman While Sailing on the Sea." The accused "capitalist-roaders" — high-level Party officials considered to be taking China in a capitalist direction — were brought onstage and lined up with their heads bowed. One by one speakers were introduced, loudspeakers blaring their voices to the crowd as they detailed the crimes of the denounced.

During the speeches, one Red Guard confided in me that his faction planned a surprise. They were going to criticize someone who wasn't onstage, Ren Zhongyi, a provincial Party secretary and the first Party secretary of Harbin — one of the province's highest-ranking officials. The way they did it was to make it look spontaneous. Onstage, one of the speakers attacked the "black provincial Party committee carrying out the revisionist line" and mentioned Ren by name. Then, by prearrangement, a group immediately began chanting, "Bring up the black gang element, Ren Zhongyi!" With seeming impatience the head of the rebel group grabbed the microphone. "In accordance with the fervent demands of the revolutionary masses, the head of the rally has decided to bring out Ren Zhongyi, the black gang element."

The audience took up the chant: "Down with the black gang element! Down with Ren Zhongyi!" as two big fellows dragged the first secretary to the stage. There they had a basin of ink, a folding chair, and a placard and a tall dunce hat, both painted with "Ren Zhongyi, black gang element," already waiting for him. That was the regular procedure in a criticism session: the denounced would be made to wear the placard and put on the paper hat, then have his face smeared with ink, and stand on a chair for public exposure.

For Ren they brought a wooden folding chair, which was very difficult to stand on. If you didn't stand in the center, it would tip over. If you stood too close to the back, the chair would fold up and collapse. So Ren needed to be very careful. The Red Guards hung the placard around his neck. Then they tried to put the one-meter-long dunce cap on his head, but the opening was too small. One Red Guard tried to force it on, but it tore. That's when another Red Guard had an idea: attach a string to the bottom of the hat and have Ren hold the other end in his hands behind his back.

The first Red Guard stepped in front of him with the basin of black ink. He asked Ren to put his hands in the basin and to smear the smelly ink over his own face. But the guard thought he hadn't smeared it enough, that he didn't look monstrous enough, so he held up the whole basin and splashed the ink over Ren's face, his eyes, his nostrils, the ink dripping from his mouth and nose all the way down to the cement floor. Another Red Guard began writing, "Down with Ren Zhongyi, the black gang element" with a brush on his white shirt. As if this were not enough, the first guard then poured half of the basin all the way down his neck, the ink dripping down from his waist, along his legs to his feet,

Li produced this panorama of Red Guards attacking Harbin's Jile Temple on 24 August 1966 by overlapping and trimming three photographs (see originals on pp. 96–97).

and coming out of his blue trousers. I was using black-and-white film, so afterward I could not distinguish between blood, tears, and ink.

All the rallies took a similar form. Generally the denounced were condemned as "capitalists," "capitalist-roaders," "counterrevolutionary revisionists," "black gang elements," or "reactionary academic authorities" — but their main crime was having power, knowledge, or wealth. Often they were condemned several times in a single day by different groups, each trying to prove themselves more revolutionary than the next. Exhausted by the torment and their imprisonment in makeshift jails — the so-called *nü pen*, or cowshed, where they were forced to stay awake at night writing confessions — they sometimes even dozed off while being condemned.

Li cropped and retouched this photograph of a rally in Harbin at the request of his editors at the *Heilongjiang Daily*. In the original (see pp. 84–85), marchers' fists seem to strike Mao's portrait; Mao's picture is in a black frame — which implies that he is dead; and the sign bearing Mao's quotation is partially obstructed by a waving flag. Li removed the fists and the black frame, and redesigned the hidden characters of the quotation.

Except for those close to the stage, most people couldn't actually see what was happening. After the speeches, they were led in shouting slogans. Then the "guilty" were put on trucks and driven around through all the major districts in town, both sides of the street flanked with crowds. Sometimes the denounced would be instructed to walk along a prescribed route wearing a placard around their neck and beating a gong. Some would be forced to do this all day long and even had to bring their lunchboxes with them. At specific spots they would have to ask a traffic policeman to sign a form to show they had complied with the order.

There was no end to the malicious inventiveness of the Red Guards. When I was in the countryside during the Socialist Education Movement, I once photographed a very famous Peking Opera singer, Yun Yanming, doing manual labor. During the Cultural Revolution she was accused of having an affair. In Chinese these women are called "worn shoes." During the height of that summer's events, I saw her on several occasions from the window of my third-floor office being paraded around by Red Guards, wearing a string of worn-out shoes dangling around her neck and a placard that said, "I am a big worn shoe."

The first time I saw Red Guards actually hitting people was in August 1966. They were condemning "capitalist-roaders" and homeowners, including Governor Li Fanwu. First they shoved their heads down. They were shouting things like, "Look at these vampires! They open their mouths and they are fed. They stretch their arms out and they are dressed!" Then the Red Guards started hitting them. One even struck the governor with the metal buckle of his military belt. But there would be worse things in store for Li Fanwu than hitting; he would be destroyed by members of his own family.

As the head of the province, the governor was a prime target of the Red Guards. He was also plotted against by his underlings, especially the younger cadres who belonged to rebel factions in the provincial government itself. They discovered that during official trips, the governor and his eldest daughter often shared the same room. They approached the governor's daughter with a sinister allegation: incest. Did they really believe the accusation? Probably not. For one, they didn't dare present the daughter in public. Instead, they wrote out a statement for her to copy. She had two choices: either sign it and receive a much sought-after army appointment, or refuse and be condemned as the daughter of a "black gang element" and sent down to the countryside. She signed the document.

On 4 September 1966, over one hundred thousand people gathered at Red Guard Square for a rally entitled "Bombard the headquarters! Expose and denounce the provincial Party committee!" The crowd was so large that it took quite a while just to get everyone to sit down. Governor Li Fanwu was taken to the stage with others and forced to bow to the waist while standing on a chair. They read his daughter's letter. Then they brought his niece onstage to reveal other "crimes." She was in her twenties and had lived with the governor and her aunt. Actually, she was brought up in his family, so she knew a lot about him. She read something prepared for her by Red Guards, exposing two major offenses: political ambition and "attempting to hide precious objects." The alleged riches were displayed at the rally: three watches, two pins, and two artificial-leather handbags. Worried about their discovery, the governor had given them to his niece for safe-keeping, but she had turned them over to the Red Guards. I looked at the watches closely. One had a worn leather band, another had a plain metal band, the third no band at all.

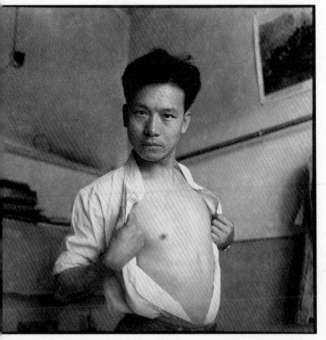

Li in his office at the *Heilongjiang Daily* in Harbin impersonates a mythical movie hero confronting his enemy and ready to fight (photographed with a self-timer). 5 June 1966

As for his political ambition, unfortunately the governor bore a striking resemblance to Mao. He once had a photo taken at the beach in Dalian that showed him with his hair swept back, wearing a trench coat and gazing toward the sea — very similar to a famous picture of Mao taken at the Chairman's summer resort on Bo Hai harbor. This picture was now introduced as evidence against him. "Comrades, look at his hairstyle, exactly like our beloved leader, Chairman Mao — so arrogant. How can we bear this?" The audience began to chant angrily: "Shave his hair. Shave his hair. Shave it into a *ghost head*."

I rushed in front of Li Fanwu and took several pictures with Mao's portrait behind so you could compare the two hairstyles. While I was taking these photographs a Red

歌舞越看越有劲

省五好职工标兵　李学义

哈尔滨之夏音乐会

向刘英俊同志学习

哈尔滨市滨江区东风公社长林大队社员　范东义

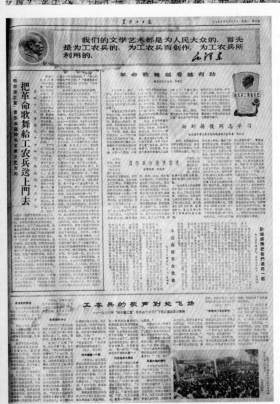

我们的文学艺术都是为人民大众的，首先是为工农兵的，为工农兵而创作，为工农兵所利用的。 毛泽东

把革命歌舞给工农兵送上门去

革命歌舞越看越有劲

向刘英俊同志学习

夏你革命歌舞选出

工农兵的歌声到处飞扬

歌颂伟大的毛泽东思想　歌颂社会主义新时代

——一九六六年"哈尔滨之夏"音乐会画页

The *Heilongjiang Daily*'s
22 August 1966 edition features
articles praising socialism's new
era and Mao Zedong Thought
(opposite bottom left), and, on
the back of the page, a pictorial
essay on Harbin's summer festival
(opposite bottom right). Red
Guards noticed that, if one held
the page against the light, a spear-
like flagpole on the top picture
of the summer festival article on
the reverse side appears to pierce
Mao's head (oposite top).
They accused the editors and the
photography team, including Li,
of having deliberately designed the
pages in a counterrevolutionary
way and of purposely insulting
Chairman Mao. A formal investigation found them guilty of
"revolutionary sloppiness."

Li checks his camera equipment
in his office at the *Heilongjiang
Daily* (photographed with a self-
timer). The sign on the door
reads, "Read Chairman Mao's
books and follow his instruction."
7 May 1966

Guard warned me to be quick or I would be considered as "blocking the revolutionary action." They were very impatient. After I stepped back, several rushed forward and without another word dragged the governor up and made him put his two hands on the back of the chair. A young man with his sleeves rolled and a female Red Guard wearing a military cap with a red star snatched the best positions, one on the right, the other on the left — both teenagers. The young man had a manual hair clipper, the girl scissors and a comb.

Without waiting for anyone's command, they took action. The young woman combed the governor's hair back off his forehead with her right hand, then cut with her left — a real "leftist," I thought. The young man made two passes over the governor's skull with the mechanical clipper, which cut very easily. Then he turned a screw on the shaver to make it more difficult. When he tried again, the governor's hair got stuck in the shaver, so he just dragged it up, tearing his hair out while talking and laughing with another young man. After a few minutes, the original hairstyle was gone, replaced by the ugly monster head. Another young female Red Guard with glasses moved forward for a turn, but most of the hair was already gone. Frustrated, she just picked up the hair lying on the stage and stuffed it down the governor's collar.

After the hair cutting, Li Fanwu was forced to stand on the chair again and to bend over down to the waist. I took another photograph, the portrait of Mao smiling behind him. His offending hair was gone, but his two criminal stains of being a "great careerist" and a "black gang element" were not removed. Nor, because of the incest allegation, was he ever truly rehabilitated. He had been a minister when the new China was founded in 1949, but he never again became more than a deputy director of a forestry bureau. And he never forgave his daughter. Not when she later knelt down at his feet and begged him. Not on his deathbed twenty years later, when in his will he barred her from attending his funeral.

During the revolution he would be criticized over two thousand times.

Because, like all Chinese newspapers, the *Heilongjiang Daily* was a branch of the local authority, the Red Guards viewed it with suspicion. A week before the attack on Jile Temple, rebels from Harbin's Military Engineering Institute and University of Industry came to the paper for a heated debate. These two universities were a breeding ground for Red Guards. The military institute was the largest university in the province, and many of the senior leaders' children studied there — including Chairman Mao's nephew.

A few days later, a rally was held at the University of Industry's sports field. Two other photographers and I were sent to cover it. When we arrived, Red Guards immediately recognized us from the debate. "You're the photojournalists for the provincial newspaper," they said. You're the *black detectives*." They thought we were there to take photographs to be later used against them, and infuriated, they surrounded us, pushing us toward the stage, trying to get us to admit that we had been sent to collect so-called black materials.

One of the photographers, the tall one, Zhang Ge, the head of the photography team, was taken up on the stage. The Red Guards demanded he answer whether he was a "black detective" or not. Zhang Ge had been a photojournalist since before the new China was founded, and I saw him raising one camera in each hand, saying, "I've been taking photographs my whole life, and if you want me to serve the people with my camera, I can try to do my best" — things like that. When the Red Guards realized they wouldn't get anything out of him, they opened his cameras and exposed all the film.

At that time, every photographer at the *Heilongjiang Daily* had a Leica M3 35 mm camera and a medium-format Rolleiflex. These two foreign-made cameras were very expensive, and in order to prevent them from being damaged, after that incident my boss bought cheaper cameras made in Shanghai and asked us to use them whenever there was a possibility of Red Guards going on a rampage. But after that event, photographers — especially the senior ones — didn't want to cover rallies and parades organized by the Red Guards.

But I was the youngest on the team. I had just come out of school. I didn't have

Li (second from left) with eight former classmates from the Changchun Film School, during an outing in Beijing in a confisctated American-made Ford Mercury formerly used by Vice Premier and Foreign Minister Chen Yi and temporarily on loan to the rebel groups from Heilongjiang province (photographed with a self-timer). 16 October 1966

that much experience, and I wanted to take as many pictures as possible. My teacher Wu Yinxian, who had taken photographs of Mao in Yanan in the 1930s, had told me once that the task of the photographer is not only to be a witness to history, but to record history — and I realized that I had to document this tumultuous period. I didn't really know whether I was doing it for the sake of the revolution, for myself, or for the future, but I knew I had to use a camera as a tool to document it.

Each month the paper only gave us fifteen rolls of 35 mm film and twenty rolls of 120 medium-format film, but for every four pictures we published, we received an extra roll of 35 mm film or two rolls of medium-format. So you had to use your head. One thing I did was stand in front of a mirror at home and shout the different slogans. I

i in his office at the *Heilongjiang
aily* dons a Red Guard arm-
and that he borowed from the
ewspaper's printing shop
hotographed with a self-timer).
July 1966

noticed that "*Jing Zhu Mao Zhuxi Wan Shou Wu
Jiang!*" — Long Live Chairman Mao — ended
with an open mouth. Good — the paper would-
n't use a picture of everyone standing there with
their fists up in the air and their mouths shut;
you needed to see them chanting. At night,
when there were big crowds but no one to lead
them, I sometimes even got them to chant this
slogan myself. As a photographer, I was also a
participant. When I wasn't taking a picture, if
the crowd chanted, I chanted; if everyone raised
their fists, I raised my fist also. Revolutionary
passions ran high, and if you didn't follow the
crowd they could easily turn on you.

I noticed, though, that people wear-
ing a Red Guard armband could take photographs freely, and quickly made up my mind
to get one. After the Cultural Revolution began, several rebel groups had formed at the
newspaper, among them the General Rebellion Group created by the editorial staff, and
the Red Workers Rebellion Group composed of workers from the printing shop. I asked to
join the editorial group, but they said I was "too conservative." I asked to join the printing group, but they told me they only took proletarian workers. One way or another,
though, I knew I had to have an armband. So on 28 August, along with five other young
men and one young woman in the editorial department, I formed a rebel group, too. Two
of the members were my roommates.

Because we only had seven members at the beginning, we couldn't call ourselves
a rebel "group." Instead, we became a "fighting team." Of course, we needed to put the
word "red" in front of it, so in the end we decided that the organization should be named
the "Red Youth Fighting Team." The other members selected me as team leader, and I
immediately went down to a shop in the street and had a red armband made with the
three characters for "Red Guard." After that, whenever I wore it I could take all the
photographs I wanted, and nobody ever bothered me.

But the members of the General Rebellion Group, who thought they were the
true red rebels at the paper, were not happy about our fighting team. In the Cultural
Revolution everyone tried to be more revolutionary than others, including myself.
Nobody wanted to be regarded as "less red." We had an argument over who were the real
revolutionaries that lasted until the beginning of 1967, when, to settle the matter, we each
selected three representatives, and the six of us took the train to Beijing and went to the

former Chinese Media Association — reorganized after the seizure of power by the rebel groups as the National Headquarters of the Red Rebels in News Media — to submit the question to their judgment.

In the end, after listening to the debate, the headquarters supported our group. We were recognized as the *real* rebels. They even gave us a new name — *Red-Color News Soldier* — and an armband with characters copied from Mao's own calligraphy. I was so excited to receive this Red-Color News Soldier armband that when I returned to Heilongjiang province I didn't even wear it. I put it away like a treasure and wore the old Red Guard one instead — and I still have it, until today. When I look at it, nearly forty years later, it is still brand-new as when it was first given to me.

The armband given to Li and his rebel group during their visit to Beijing at the end of 1966. Individual characters copied from Mao's calligraphy were assembled to read, "Red-Color News Soldier." The armband bears the official stamp of the "National Headquarters of the Revolutionary Rebels in News Media."

1966

On 16 May 1966, Mao issued the document that officially launched the Great Proletarian Cultural Revolution. Rejecting a more limited resolution made three months earlier, the May 16 Notice asserted that "The whole Party must follow Comrade Mao Zedong's instructions, hold high the great banner of the proletarian Cultural Revolution, thoroughly expose the reactionary bourgeois stand of those so-called academic authorities who oppose the Party and socialism, thoroughly criticize and repudiate the reactionary bourgeois ideas in the sphere of academic work, education, journalism, literature and art, and publishing, and seize the leadership in these cultural spheres. To achieve this," the document added ominously, "it is necessary at the same time to criticize and repudiate those representatives of the bourgeoisie who have sneaked into the Party, the government, the army, and all spheres of culture, to clear them out. . ."

The announcement coincided with the birth of the Red Guard at a middle school in Beijing. Marked by a fierce devotion to "die fighting to protect Chairman Mao" and inflamed by his exhortations to "start fires" to keep the revolutionary spirit alive, members of the grassroots student movement placarded the nation's walls with slogans and personal handwritten statements called "big character posters" held rallies, attacked teachers and all forms of authority, and quickly clashed with government authorities. President Liu Shaoqi vainly pleaded for instructions from the Chairman before sending in work teams to the schools to restore order. But after the work teams restrained the violence on the campuses, Mao seized on the action as a pretext to launch an attack on the "bourgeois headquarters" headed by Liu, and began to make his way back to Beijing.

On 16 July 1966, a seventy-two-year-old Mao went for a swim in the Yangtze River in a two-hour public display of vigor that signaled he was back at the helm. Two days later he flew to Beijing. Forcing Liu Shaoqi's public self-criticism for having carried out an "act of oppression and terror," on 5 August Mao took a cue from the Red Guards and wrote his own big character poster. It said, "Bombard the Headquarters!" Having fought the Nationalists, the Japanese, the Americans and the Soviets, landlords and capitalists, the man who had once written that "politics is war by other means" now set in motion a guerrilla assault on his own Party.

Harbin, Heilongjiang province, 1 June 1966

A joyous crowd takes to the streets
at night after an official broadcast
publicizes the contents of a big
character poster hung on 25 May
at Beijing University denouncing
Party leaders at the school
for failing to carry out the Cultural
Revolution.

Several thousand faculty members and students from Harbin's University of Industry take to the streets to celebrate Mao's first meeting with citizens supporting the Cultural Revolution, holding aloft a panel that reads, "Care about the affairs of state and carry out the Great Proletarian Cultural Revolution until the end."

Harbin, 12 August 1966

On the night of 13 August, people take to the streets to celebrate the Central Committee's adoption of the "Sixteen Points" — a blueprint for the Cultural Revolution (below). Three days later, Red Guards rename Harbin's fashionable Madier restaurant, with its European-inspired architecture, "Anti-revisionist Restaurant" (opposite).

Harbin, 13–16 August 1966

Harbin, 17 August 1966

The revolutionary fervor of the Red Guards is unleashed against the Party establishment at a mass rally held at Red Guard Square calling for the "burning of the North-eastern Bureau" (large characters in center).

On 18 August 1966 Mao stood atop Tiananmen Gate in Beijing before a million cheering Red Guards waving Little Red Books and pinned on an armband presented to him by a young female Red Guard. With this gesture he decisively threw his weight behind the student movement and against the entrenched Party establishment. Within weeks, this symbolic act reverberated throughout China, spawning thousands of rebel groups under no one's direct control, widespread demonstrations, epic criticism sessions, and a nation-wide wave of violence.

Under the banner of eliminating the "four olds" — old thought, old culture, old customs, and old practices — school officials, news-paper editors, intellectuals, and bureaucrats from all levels of gov-ernment were attacked and often overthrown in a revolutionary mael-strom as the campaign to eradicate all "snake monsters and ox demons" slowly made its way up the ranks of the Party hierarchy.

In Heilongjiang, the Cultural Revolution brought to power Pan Fusheng. A former first Party secretary of Henan province in the late 1950s, Pan had lost his position by opposing Mao's Great Leap Forward, and was reassigned as chairman of a marketing coopera-tive in Beijing. Anxious to prove his loyalty to the Chairman, he subsequently embraced an ultraleftist line and in 1966 was rewarded with an appointment as the new first Party secretary of Heilongjiang. By the end of August 1966, with his public support, Red Guards organized demonstrations of hundreds of thousands of people in the capital city of Harbin, renamed streets, stadiums, and restaurants with new revolutionary names, conducted household searches, and confined, beat, and tormented those deemed ene-mies. Classes in schools were suspended, and industry came to a virtual standstill as the entire population was required to follow the crowd and join in the revolutionary events.

Red Guards perform the "It is Right to Rebel" song and dance (below). The newly appointed first secretary of the provincial Party committee, Pan Fusheng, addresses a crowd wearing a Red Guard armband, encouraging them to "rebel against the provincial Party leadership" (opposite).

Harbin, 22–23 August 1966

Harbin, 23 August 1966

Provincial Party Secretary Wang Yilun, one of Heilongjiang's most powerful leaders, is criticized by Red Guards from the University of Industry and forced to bear a placard around his neck with the accusation "counterrevolutionary revisionist element."

Harbin, 23–24 August 1966

Red Guards attack Saint Nicholas, the wooden Russian Orthodox church (opposite), before tearing it to pieces. The next day, they ransack the Buddhist Jile Temple, burning sculptures and holy scriptures (below).

Among the many enemies of the Red Guards was a familiar nemesis of communism: religion. Traditional Buddhism, long tolerated by the communists, as well as the imported religion of Christianity, now came under attack as temples and churches were looted and destroyed, holy books and statues desecrated, and religious leaders condemned. In Harbin, at the height of the summer's frenzy, mobs pulled down the venerated hundred-year-old wooden Russian Orthodox church of Saint Nicholas with the help of a fire truck and rope, and the following day ransacked the city's famous center of Buddhism, the venerable Paradise (Jile) Temple.

Masses gathered in front of the Jile Temple cheer as Red Guards from the Harbin Military Institute force self-criticism on the monks after vandalizing their sanctuary.

Harbin, 24 August 1966

Harbin, 24 August 1966

As part of the monks' self-criticism, they are forced to hold a banner that reads, "To hell with the Buddhist scriptures. They are full of dog farts."

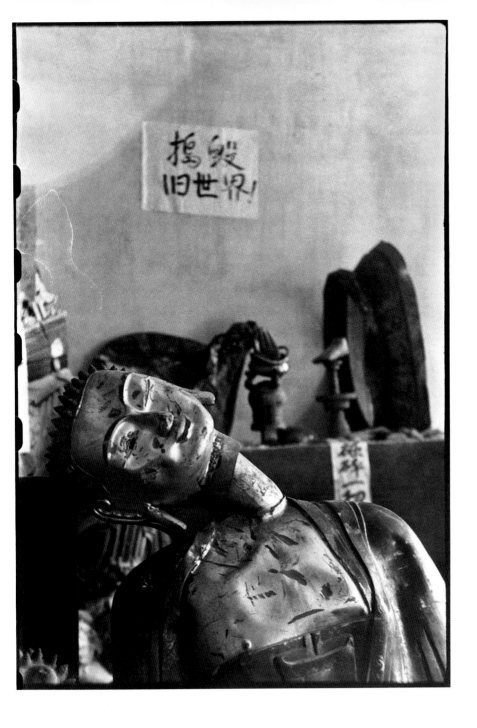

Harbin, 24 August 1966

In the aftermath of the destruction of the Jile Temple, a sign posted on the wall reads, "smash the old world" (opposite), and damaged statues are desecrated with paper dunce caps (above).

Harbin, 25 August 1966

The staff of the *Heilongjiang Daily*
accuses Luo Zicheng, head of
the work group designated by the
provincial Party committee,
of following the capitalist line and
opposing the mass movement.
His dunce cap announces his
crimes, and on the wall behind him
are portraits of Mao, Liu Shaoqi,
Zhou Enlai, Zhu De, Chen Yun,
Lin Biao, and Deng Xiaoping
(from left to right).

By late August 1966, the struggle sessions of the Socialist Education Movement had evolved into sadistic spectacles of cruelty attended by hundreds of thousands. The denounced, their faces smeared with ink, were now forced to bow for hours while standing on chairs, and to wear grotesquely elongated dunce caps and placards with their names crossed out. Afterward, they would be paraded through town on the backs of flatbed trucks. Some would be imprisoned in makeshift prisons called the *nü pen* — or cowshed — and removed only to be taken from one criticism to the next, denounced hundreds, in some cases even thousands of times.

As in the rest of China, the primary targets of the Red Guards in Heilongjiang were the government and the provincial Party committee. The escalating criticisms soon reached their top leaders: Ren Zhongyi, a provincial Party secretary and first Party secretary of Harbin, and Li Fanwu, provincial Party secretary and governor of Heilongjiang. In massive rallies at Harbin's People's Stadium, which had recently been renamed Red Guard Square, the two, along with other Party secretaries, were set onstage, accused of a myriad of often shamelessly fabricated crimes, heaped with abuse, and physically tormented by zealous Red Guards.

Harbin, 26 August 1966

At a rally in Red Guard Square, provincial Party secretary and first Party secretary of Harbin Ren Zhongyi, after having his face smeared with black ink, is forced to wear a dunce cap and a placard around his neck with the accusatory label "black gang element" while standing on an unstable chair with his hands behind his back holding a string attached to the ill-fitting hat.

Harbin, 29 August 1966

a mass rally organized by rebels
Provincial People's Stadium,
arty Secretary Wang Yilun and Li
a, the wife of Governor Li Fanwu,
e denounced, their faces and
othes splattered with ink, and
eir crimes spelled out on plac-
rds around their necks (opposite);
enounced Vice-Governor Chen
ejing is paraded through the
owd (below).

Top Party officials are denounced during an afternoon-long rally in Red Guard Square: Li Fanwu (top, right), provincial Party secretary and governor of Heilongjiang, is criticized as a "careerist," while Wang Yilun (above, left) is accused of being a "black gang element." That same day another provincial Party secretary, Chen Lei, is denounced at Provincial People's Stadium (opposite).

Harbin, 29 August 1966

In addition to "hoarding riches," Governor Li Fanwu was alleged to have committed incest with his eldest daughter. Characteristic of the way the Cultural Revolution turned children against their parents, she was coerced into making the accusation herself, offered the choice of being branded the child of a "black gang element" and exiled to hard labor in the countryside if she refused, or provided with a sought-after position in the army if she agreed. Ultimately she copied and signed a statement prepared by Red Guards exposing her father's "crime." Li Fanwu was also accused of political ambition. Evidence for this was found in his hairstyle, which gave him an ill-fated resemblance to Mao and so was said to symbolize his lust for power. Amid cries of "Shave his hair. Shave it into a *ghost head*," two young Red Guards brutally chopped off his hair. Once one of the most powerful men in the province, the governor would be criticized over two thousand times during the Cultural Revolution. He survived but, forever tainted by the salacious accusation of incest, would never be truly rehabilitated.

Accused of bearing a resemblance to Mao, Heilongjiang province Governor Li Fanwu's hair is brutally shaved and torn by zealous young Red Guards in Red Guard Square

Harbin, 12 September 1966

Harbin, 12 September 1966

After having his hair torn out, Li Fanwu is made to bow for hours, clippings of his hair stuffed down his neck and shirt by an infuriated Red Guard. The banner behind him reads, "Bombard the Headquarters! Expose and denounce the provincial Party committee."

Evidence of Li Fanwu's crime of "hoarding riches" is displayed: three watches, two brooches, and three artificial-leather handbags. Li Fanwu's niece, who had promised to hold on to the belongings, turned them over to the Red Guards.

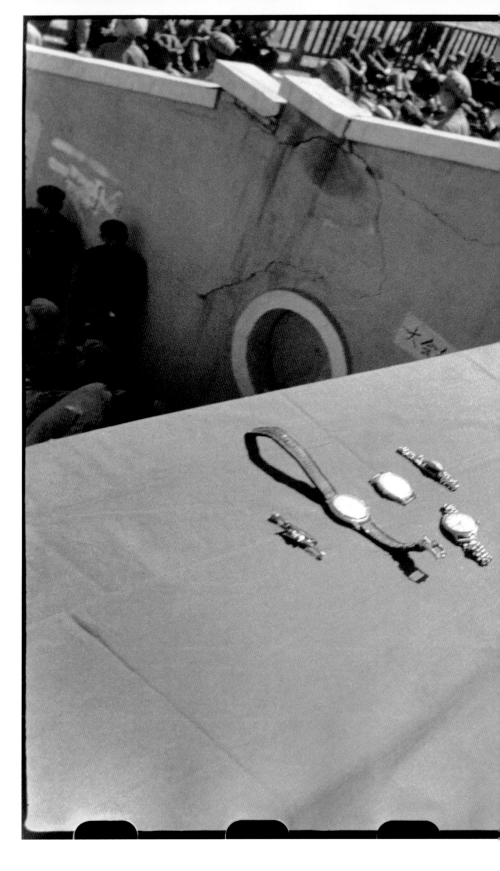

Harbin, 12 September 1966

Harbin, 12 September 1966

After a month of criticism sessions, Lü Qi'en, the mayor of Harbin (opposite, far left), Chen Lei, Li Fanwu, and Wang Yilun (opposite and above, right to left) are paraded through the streets of Harbin in trucks, their names and accusations – counterrevolutionary, local despot, and black gang element — prominently displayed on placards around their necks.

Harbin, 13 September 1966

During a propaganda-movie
screening in a Harbin cinema, the
audience of students applauds,
shouting "Long Live Chairman
Mao" each time his image appears
on-screen (here followed
by Defense Minister Lin Biao).

Several hundred thousand people attend a "Learning and Applying Mao Zedong Thought" rally in Red Guard Square.

Harbin, 13 September 1966

Harbin, 19 September 1966

Ziwen, accused of being a "big
operty owner," is forced to carry
chair onto the stage at Red
uard Square and to stand on it
public criticism. The placard
und her neck bears her name
d her crime.

124   Harbin, 19 September–1 October 1966

tocks, securities certificates, and
avings-deposit books confiscated
  home searches are burned
  a rally led by Red Guards
pposite). On National Day,
choolchildren carrying red-tassled
ears and wearing Red Guard
rmbands parade through
e streets past a Russian-style
epartment store (above).

Beijing, 5 October 1966

Stoking the flames of the new revolution ever higher, Mao made eight appearances before the Red Guards in Beijing's Tiananmen Square between August and November of 1966. With Red Guards granted free rail travel, these events attracted more than eleven million from all over China. The result were orgies of Mao devotion, marked by a sea of green uniforms, red armbands, and Little Red Books, as troupes of Red Guards danced the "Loyalty Dance" and sang revolutionary songs like "Rely on the Helmsman While Sailing the Seas" and "The Sun in the East," sometimes waiting weeks for a glimpse of their Great Leader.

These appearances represented the crescendo of the phenomenon known as the cult of Mao. Though seemingly at odds with communism's goal to establish a classless society, Mao, like Stalin before him, understood the power of celebrity and used it, consolidating power around his own burgeoning myth.

Amid a crowd of over one million Red Guards assembled in Tiananmen Square awaiting Mao's appearance, one group dances the "Loyalty Dance."

A young Red Guard performs
the "Loyalty Dance" while
awaiting Mao's appearance in
Tiananmen Square.

Beijing, 18 October 1966

III.

At the end of September 1966, I went to Beijing to cover the "big networking" of the Red Guards and Chairman Mao's fifth appearance before them in Tiananmen Square. Mao would review the Red Guards eight times between August and November of that year, receiving over eleven million altogether, and this was the biggest gathering yet, with well over a million and a half of the faithful pouring into the capital, the "center of world revolution," from all over the country to catch a glimpse of the Great Helmsman.

I accompanied the rebel groups from the Harbin Military Engineering Institute. The whole trip — transportation, lodging, meals — was arranged by the central government, and it was all free. A special train took us directly from Harbin to Beijing. Once there, the students slept in middle schools on makeshift beds made out of tables. Journalists from the *Heilongjiang Daily*, including myself, stayed at a small hotel near the front gate of Tiananmen Square.

After National Day on 1 October, Red Guards filled the square day and night, waiting for Mao. They knew he would review them sometime soon, but didn't know exactly when; this information was always kept secret until the last moment. In the meantime, zealous guards made passionate speeches promoting Mao Zedong Thought, sang revolutionary songs, and tirelessly danced the "Loyalty Dance."

Finally, on the evening of 17 October, the loudspeakers announced that Mao would make his appearance the following day. At the news a surge of excitement swept through the crowd, and everyone stayed up all night celebrating. I was excited, too, and only slept a couple of hours. Then at dawn we were loaded on trucks and taken to Fuxing Road, to the west of Tiananmen Square. There we waited, organized in tight formation, very disciplined. We were asked to make sure we recognized all the people around us and to report any strangers. We waited a long time. Then, sometime after noon, we heard an electrifying hail coming from down the road: "Long live Chairman Mao!"

A few days earlier I had come to Tiananmen with my camera. After making tests on an approaching car, I knew that from the moment Mao's vehicle became visible to the moment of its passing, I could shoot three to five frames. I'll get at least one good shot, I thought; Mao in high spirits and his trademark smile that was always reported in the news, the "glorious image of Chairman Mao" — that's what I thought I'd capture. But I was shocked to see the jeep with Mao approaching in my viewfinder. The Red Guards were hailing him from both sides of the road, hot tears in their eyes — but I didn't see the so-called glorious image. Mao did not wave or smile. He looked straight ahead, expressionless. He held his hands as if clapping. But he wasn't clapping. The jeep was moving very fast. If I didn't act quickly, I would miss it. I pressed the shutter. One frame. That was the first and last time I ever saw Mao Zedong.

Front page of the *Heilongjiang Daily*, 6 April 1968. The vertical calligraphy on the right is in Lin Biao's own hand: "Rely on the Helmsman while sailing the seas; rely on Mao Zedong Thought while making revolution."

131

Li (center) in Tiananmen Square
in Beijing with colleagues
from the *Heilongjiang Daily*
shortly after Mao's fifth appearance before the Red Guards
(photograph by Xin Hua).
20 October 1966

People in China began studying Mao's work in the early 1960s, before the Cultural Revolution began — as one can see from the photographs I took during the "four cleanups" movement. At the beginning, I was sincere in reading his work, too — that is, some of it made sense to me. Mao had the quality of always striving to become stronger and better. If he couldn't arrive somewhere directly, he would arrive there indirectly. There is a saying in China: "The skies won't open up without whimsical thinking." That's how Mao was — and that's how, with fewer men and weapons, he defeated the Nationalists. Chiang Kai-shek thought he could root Mao out from Yanan in three months. But Mao dared to think, to set up goals, to strive to meet them. If he hadn't, he would have remained a schoolteacher in Hunan province.

The thing is, later on people regarded Mao as a god, and whatever he said became like scripture. That was the social atmosphere then. Mao was more than a leader. He was our *savior*. And everyone had to believe — or pretend to. His instructions were holy writ and needed to be obeyed blindly. Lin Biao, Mao's second in command and the force behind the Little Red Book, put it this way: "Chairman Mao is a genius . . . One single sentence of his surpasses ten thousand of ours." But if you look at the photographs I took, you can see that I was already beginning to have my own judgment about what was going on. For example, when people turned Mao's slogans into songs and sang them enthusiastically; when I took a photograph of that kind of scene, consciously or unconsciously I frequently tried to choose angles or compositions that showed it was all a bit crazy to me.

At the time, altering news photographs was a requirement of the political situation, too. For example, I once took a picture of two people reading the Little Red Book.

There was a portrait of Mao behind them on the wall. Shooting with the aperture fully open, the foreground was sharp and the portrait behind slightly blurry. But such was the reverence for the Great Helmsman that you couldn't publish a blurry portrait. So I had to find a sharp picture of Mao and superimpose it over the soft one. Even more illogically, another time I made a picture of a crowded rally at a sports field from behind, so you couldn't see all the portraits held up, only their wooden frames — and for the final image, my editor instructed me to add pictures of Mao to the back of the frames, even though this skewed the perspective and it made no sense that they were facing the wrong way.

In cases like this I did much of the retouching and manipulation myself — and actually I was quite good at it; I kept dozens of portraits of Mao in all sorts of sizes under the glass on my desk handy for just such purposes, and my years of training in painting really helped me when I had to complete a blocked slogan or paint out someone's fist that looked as though it were striking our great Leader's face.

After I returned from Beijing with the Red-Color News Soldier armband at the beginning of 1967, the "Revolutionary Rebel Headquarters of Workers" in Shanghai overthrew the municipal Party committee and the government. That spear-heading event was called the "January Storm," and the storm swept all over China.

On 10 January, Red Guards from both Harbin's Military Engineering Institute and Teacher's College took over the *Heilongjiang Daily* and shut it down. The next day, there was no newspaper. For the five days after that, only wire stories from the Xinhua News Agency were published; no local news, not even the paper's masthead at the top. The day-to-day management was put in the hands of the deputy editors in chief, who had yet to be denounced. The Red Guards, looking for a group to represent them at the paper, in the end chose the Red Rebel League — an alliance led by my Red Youth

Reeducation scene from Xinsheng commune in which a dancer reads Mao's works with an elderly peasant woman in Qingan county, Heilongjiang province, on November 1969. The original picture (right) was retouched prior to publication in order to show an unobstructed and sharply focused portrait of Mao on a cleaned-up background (far right).

i travels by plane for the first
me, accompanying Pan Fusheng
nd the delegation from the
feilongjiang revolutionary
ommittee to Beijing to report
n the situation in the province
photograph by Fan Zhengmei).
5 March 1967

ront pages from the *Heilongjiang
aily*, opposite clockwise from
p left: On 9 January 1968 the
eadline reads, "Chairman Mao's
test instructions," and the
haracters in the red box at bottom
all on all to "Thoroughly imple-
ent our great leader Chairman
fao's latest instructions and look
rward to the victory of the Great
roletarian Cultural Revolution."
n 7 April 1968 the headline
roclaims, "The sun illuminates
very corner of Heilongjiang
rovince. Every red heart turns
oward to the red sun." On 1 August
968 the paper celebrates PLA
ay with a vertical headline,
Long live Chairman Mao, Great
ommander and founder of
he Chinese People's Liberation
army." On 29 April 1968 the
eadline invokes all to "Set off
mong the masses a new upsurge
f learning and applying
hairman Mao's works. Vow to
urn our province into a great red
chool of Mao Zedong Thought."

Fighting Team. They thought we were younger and purer than the other groups.

My main purpose in forming a rebel faction had originally been to get an armband — but suddenly I found myself thrust to the forefront of the rebellion. The first thing we did was to set up a big character poster condemning the paper and the editor in chief, Zhao Yang as revisionist. Then we held criticism sessions. These sessions were a way of purging the "bourgeois line of thinking" considered especially prevalent in the arts and media. Before the Cultural Revolution, the editor in chief had a fancy Russian car, a Volga, and a chauffeur; the deputy editors in chief shared a Polish car, a Warsaw, and they all had big houses. After the criticisms, they had to move to smaller homes and ride in the shuttle bus with the rest of us.

At the *Heilongjiang Daily*, these sessions took place in a big conference room. There, I helped conduct one denouncing Zhao, the man who had watched me walk back and forth the day I was hired. Was he angry with me afterward? If so, it was subtle. Later, I heard that he actually preferred my criticism session to the others because at least I did it "according to the policy" — by this he meant that there was no fighting, no hitting in my meetings; that I would try to maintain order when people got over-excited and started saying, "Let's also criticize so and so!" The groups representing the workers, by contrast, were much more passionate. The printers and truckers represented two-thirds of the paper's staff, and they would violently force down the heads of the denounced, whereas I would just say, "Bow your head." That's part of the reason my group was overthrown so quickly. We were regarded as too conservative, as a faction "protecting the emperor."

The groups waged a bitter feud. One day that January, my roommate, who was also a member of our fighting team, raced up to me all out of breath. "The workers' rebel group has stormed the editorial department!" he cried. "They are attacking the arts-section editor, Ru Weiran!"

When I arrived, I saw Ru standing on a chair placed atop a table, his head almost touching the ceiling. The workers, led by a man nicknamed "Red Beard," had tied a rope around the leg of the chair so they could topple him at any moment. His crime? Ru was also a well-known poet. But generally less educated, the workers couldn't really understand his poems and considered them "reactionary."

Ru looked down and saw me. "Zhensheng, save me," he pleaded meekly. I knew I had to be careful — to keep Ru from getting his neck broken without upsetting the ardent

Li (seated, center) leads a criticism session against rival rebel group supporter Fan Changwu (standing, left) at the *Heilongjiang Daily* in Harbin on 19 February 1967 (photograph by Wan Jiyao). Less than two years later Li himself would be criticized in the same conference room.

workers. After a moment, I loudly asked: "Ru Weiran, do you admit that your poems are reactionary?" "Yes," he murmured. "I didn't hear you!" I shouted. A glint of fear shone in Ru's eyes. "Ru Weiran, come down and publicly admit it to the revolutionary workers so they can hear you!" "Yes!" he cried, his voice trembling. "I will!" The workers looked on approvingly, their passions momentarily sated, and Ru climbed down.

On 31 January 1967, Heilongjiang became the first province in China to replace its Party committee with a revolutionary committee. At the paper, a six-member "standing commission of the revolutionary committee" was put in charge. As members they chose a driver, two student Red Guards, two editors, and myself. I became chief of staff and the deputy commander of the political-affairs unit. I was given an office, a secretary, and the committee seal. I had changed from an ordinary journalist to someone with power — and I was filled with a sense of self-contentment.

That April, the provincial revolutionary committee sent four representatives from the PLA — the People's Liberation Army — to the newspaper. Everything was given a military structure: the editorial department was renamed the editorial-affairs platoon, and one of the PLA representatives was selected as chairman of the standing commission, replacing a Red Guard who had decided to return to the university.

As a member of the commission, I tried to conduct my duties without cruelty. One day a man named Luo approached my secretary for a letter certifying he worked at the newspaper so that his wife could get a job. His wife was applying for work in a boiler room, which paid something like eighteen *yuan* a month. Luo, however, had been condemned during the anti-rightist campaign in 1957 and sent to reform through hard labor.

My secretary made a reference to this in the letter. When Luo read it, he came to me and said that with a letter like this, his wife would never be able to find a job. I simply crossed out this line and asked my secretary to rewrite it. I'm not saying I'm very noble. Only I had some compassion. I belonged to a rebel faction, but I never hit anybody. Instead I was hit. I didn't search anyone's home. Instead my own house was searched.

Like everyone else at the time, I rid myself of "suspect" belongings, such as an edition of love poems by Pushkin and a book of paintings by Xu Beihong, who had studied in France and was criticized during the Cultural Revolution for his nudes. I also hid under my bed three stamps of works by Goya, including his painting *Naked Maya*, and some old silver coins with the likenesses of Chiang Kai-shek and the self-proclaimed emperor Yuan Shikai. Everyone looked very revolutionary from the outside, but deep down, it was often another story.

In any political movement, as in normal times, people still fall in love. My girl-friend from film school, Sun Peikui, had decided not to become an actress after all, and transferred to another school to study Chinese instead. After graduating, she was assigned to teach at a high school on the outskirts of Siping, a city in Jilin province. She had been selected as a model teacher by both the municipal and the provincial authori-ties, but during the Cultural Revolution her mother was condemned for being brought up in a landlord family and, tormented, committed suicide.

Those who committed suicide — and there were countless during the Cultural Revolution — were regarded as having "alienated themselves from the people and the Party." Overnight Peikui's life changed. She, too, was criti-cized and condemned. She was called the daughter of a "dog landlord" who had "infiltrated the teachers' ranks," a "fake model," and made to attend study sessions where she was investigated and spent endless hours poring over Mao's works. Her room in the dormitory for singles was wrecked, and she was forced to share a room with a married couple she knew, lying in the same bed — even when they made love.

Ironically, Sun Peikui was an adopted child — but it didn't matter. The same way it didn't matter that her mother, who would be rehabilitated after the Cultural Revolution, hadn't come from a landlord family at all.

In April Peikui came to Harbin. I showed her around the city a little, but she was in no mood for

photographs his girlfriend n Peikui in her apartment in ping, Jilin province. Peikui lost r position as a schoolteacher ter her mother, criticized as elonging to a landlord family," mmitted suicide. 2 May 1967

sight-seeing. Crying, she told me what had happened. She said we could not be married, that I was a member of the standing commission and had a bright future and that she didn't want to create problems for me. Visiting the newspaper, she also couldn't help noticing Zu Yingxia, a young female editor. Yingxia was smart and pretty and one of the founding members of the Red Youth Fighting Team. She also belonged to the Communist Party. Peikui suggested I marry her instead.

Li in his office at the newspaper with his future wife, Zu Yingxia, an editor and member of Li's rebel group the "Red Youth Fighting Team" (photographed with a self-timer). 20 August 196

"Let's go live in the forest," I pleaded with her. "If your family background won't allow me to be a journalist, then I won't be a journalist. We'll set up a home somewhere in the remote mountainous regions." But Peikui knew it would never work. Even there, people would ask us for our household registration certificate and where we had come from. Local authorities in China were expert at getting reports from every corner of the country.

Peikui left without saying good-bye. I found a note waiting for me in my room. "It's because I love you that I don't want to destroy you," she said. "I want us to part — I want you to forget me." After I read the letter, I ran all the way to the railway station, but I didn't see her anywhere. So I caught the next train to Siping where she lived, and went to her apartment to try and change her mind. I told her it would be alright, that it would all work out. But Peikui did not agree. Two months later, she sent me a letter with a photograph from her wedding. She had married a neighbor from her hometown. This man had courted her before film school. He was not good-looking and no taller than she was. He worked in Changchun, in auto manufacturing, and she only became his wife so I would give up hope. She had "only married a man," she wrote, "not a lover."

Yingxia and I were married six months later, on 6 January 1968 — a typical revolutionary wedding. With wicked black humor, some of our friends hung placards around our necks. Instead of "capitalist-roader" or "black-gang element," the signs read, "Groom taking the socialist road" and "Bride taking the socialist road." But if the Cultural Revolution had not taken place, I know Peikui and I would have wed.

As it happened, ten months later Yingxia's father committed suicide, too. He was a country doctor in a commune clinic, famous for his knowledge of traditional medicine, but he was denounced as a "reactionary academic authority." One night, some rebels placed him in front of a coal-burning stove until he was drenched with sweat, then forced him to strip down to his underclothes and sent him outdoors to stand in the snow until he was nearly frozen. The following day he hanged himself.

When Yingxia found out, she burst into tears. But she didn't have time to grieve. She washed her face and, with her eyes still swollen, reported to the propaganda-team representative at the paper. For the sake of her own future, she couldn't show any emotion. "My father has betrayed the Cultural Revolution," she said. "And I want to 'draw a line' between him and myself." Even so, afterward Yingxia — like Peikui — was considered "politically unreliable" and forced to attend study sessions. She had been thought one of the best editors at the paper, but after her father's suicide she was no longer allowed to work in the editorial department at all.

•

Three months after our wedding, on 5 April 1968, I photographed an execution of seven men and one woman. Six — including the woman and her lover, who had murdered her husband — were "ordinary" criminals. The other two men were technicians at the Harbin Electric Meter Factory who had published a flyer entitled "Looking North," which the authorities interpreted as "looking northward toward Soviet revisionism." They were condemned as counterrevolutionaries. One was named Wu Bingyuan, and when he heard the sentence, he looked into the sky and murmured, "This world is too dark"; then he closed his eyes and never in this life reopened them. All eight were put on the backs of trucks in pairs, driven through town, then out to the countryside northwest of Harbin. There, on the barren grounds of the Huang Shan Cemetery, they were lined up, hands tied behind their backs, and forced to kneel. They were all shot in the back of the head.

's wedding celebration in a con-
rence room of the *Heilongjiang*
aily. His colleagues playfully
ang criticism-type placards
round the newlyweds' necks that
ad: "Groom taking the socialist
ad" and "Bride taking the
cialist road" (photograph by
u Qixiang). 6 January 1968

Li in his office holding his
Rolleiflex (photographed with
another medium-format camera
set on a self-timer). 17 July 1967

No one asked me to take close-ups of the bodies, but that's what I did, and because I had only a 35 mm wide-angle lens, I had to get very close, so close I could smell the fishy smell of blood and brains.

For the next six months, I couldn't get their faces out of my mind. At that time, Yingxia and I still hadn't been provided with an apartment and lived separately in the dorm. The toilet was at the end of a long corridor, and whenever I woke up at night needing to go to the bathroom, I would walk with my eyes closed, trying not to bump into the shoes and small stoves left outside the doors on both sides of the hallway and trying not to think of the dead. When I ate in the cafeteria and they served a local dish like blood tofu, which was red and gelatinous, I felt like vomiting.

As I enlarged the photographs of these executed people in the dim red light of the darkroom, I quietly spoke to them. I told them, "If your souls are haunted, please don't haunt me, too. I'm only trying to help. I'm making your pictures because I want to record history. I want people to know that you were wronged." And until this day — even when I printed the images for this book in New York — I always say that.

1966–1968

After waiting for days in and around Tiananmen Square for a glimpse of the Great Helmsman, crowds cheer and wave Little Red Books as he passes in his jeep. Mao is standing behind the driver; behind him is his personal physician, Li Zhisui; to Mao's left is General Yang Chengwu; and beside the driver is Mao's chief of staff, Wang Dongxing.

Beijing, 18 October 1966

By the fall of 1966 Mao had become, to most Chinese, a living god. Popular songs like "The Sun in the East" and newspaper editorials extolled his limitless virtues, while millions traveled to the capital, Beijing, from all over the country, sometimes on foot, for just a glimpse of the Great Helmsman. Mao's elevation to superhuman status was all the more remarkable considering that his previous mass movement — the Great Leap Forward — had resulted in the famine-related death of over twenty million people.

Mao managed such sweeping control over the country through a propaganda campaign of unprecedented scope. Carefully coordinated by his new second in command, Marshal Lin Biao, the force behind the Little Red Book, and the Chairman's wife, Jiang Qing, who wielded her power over all aspects of culture and media, the cult of Mao splashed the Great Leader's "supreme instructions" onto the walls of every factory and across every newspaper page, and put his likeness into every home on posters, buttons, fabrics, and dishes. Two seemingly contradictory forces fueled the cult, as Mao was simultaneously ever-present (in image) and inaccessible (in person). With the exception of those who attended one of Mao's eight reviews of the Red Guards at Tiananmen Square between August and November 1966, few Chinese ever saw him. And although Mao Zedong Thought had become the ubiquitous official expression of Chinese thinking, replacing nearly all other writing, much of which was now banned, nearly one-third of all Chinese were still unable to read.

The overall effect was to make Mao one of the most powerful men on the planet, puppet master of a swirl of destruction and fear from which he alone was immune. Schools shut down, and industry slowed to a crawl as rebels turned on capitalists, religious leaders, the press, local Party leadership, and each other. By the summer of 1967, the violence had reached its peak. Marauding Red Guards conducted random household searches, ransacked libraries, and held interrogations as millions were killed, tortured, or committed suicide before Mao finally sent in the PLA (People's Liberation Army) to pull the country back from the brink of total chaos.

Beijing, 18 October 1966

The procession following Mao's
Jeep carry his would-be successor,
Vice-Chairman Marshal Lin Bao
(top), Premier Zhou Enlai (center),
and Mao's wife, Jiang Qing
(bottom).

Shi Shouyun, an elated teenage Red Guard, records in her Little Red Book the exact time she "met with" Chairman Mao as he rode by in his motorcade near Tiananmen Square.

Beijing, 18 October 1966

National conferences such as this one on "Learning and Applying Mao Zedong Thought," held in Beijing's Workers' Stadium (below), were a common way of spreading Maoist thought. The mass-produced Mao portraits displayed at the national conference are identical to the one a peasant from Acheng county exhibits to his neighbors (opposite).

Beijing, 21 October 1966; Acheng county, Heilongjiang province, 2 November 1966

Harbin, Heilongjiang province, 9 November–10 December 1966

At the Harbin Worker's Club, Party
secretaries Chen Lei, Wang Yilun,
and Li Fanwu (opposite, left to right)
are forced to wear oversized paper
dunce caps during a criticism
session. In the Binjiang district, a
newlywed couple decorate their
bedroom with pictures and quotations of Mao (above). Later criticized
for making love under the eyes of
their leader, they asserted that they
always first turned out the lights.

Having overthrown numerous Party leaders, intellectuals, and other "demons and monsters," by early 1967 the tens of thousands of Red Guard and rebel groups whose destructive force Mao had harnessed to wage revolution turned on one another. The period of infighting that followed produced some of the most violent episodes of the Cultural Revolution, as rivals armed themselves, clashed in pitched battles, and took prisoners in a fight for the power and prestige that went with being acknowledged as the "real" revolutionaries.

Generally the factions shared a similar ideology: total support for Mao and a willingness to "die fighting." But fissures among the Chairman's grassroots shock troops developed along class lines, according to family background, and between those who wanted to preserve a refashioned Party leadership and those who wished to destroy all power structures. This conflict between "radicals" and "emperor protectors" was endlessly reenacted on campuses and in workplaces throughout the country. As Mao wrote the following year, "Except in the deserts, at every place of human habitation there is the left, the center, and the right. This will continue to be so ten thousand years hence."

On the steps of Harbin's North Plaza Hotel, which served as a public space for criticism sessions and Red Guard rallies, one rebel group forces leaders from a rival group to kneel and be criticized.

Harbin, 17 January 1967

153

Harbin, 18–19 January 1967

wo leaders of a rebel faction are
scorted to the front of the North
aza Hotel where they are forced
 kneel on the ground during
public denunciation (opposite).
he following day Hao Deren,
cused of forming an armed
oup to establish a so-called Red
ag Army of China, is taken
 be denounced at the same
cation (above).

Harbin, 31 January–2 February 1967

n 31 January 1967, Heilongjiang became the first of China's twenty-
ne provinces to replace its government and Party committee with
new revolutionary committee. The rest of the country would soon
llow suit. From the highest levels of government in Beijing to
oduction brigades in the countryside, the old guard was
estroyed. But having achieved full control of the government and
rty apparatus through anarchy, Mao now made certain that the
archy itself was controlled and the apparatus protected.
ccordingly, he initiated the "three-in-one alliance," in which power
the revolutionary committees governing the country would be
ared by rebels, veteran cadres, and, most important, the PLA
eople's Liberation Army). The army, which had greatly expanded
influence since the replacement of denounced President Liu
aoqi with the deputy commander of the army, Lin Biao, received
e most important seats on the new committees.

e founding of Heilongjiang's
volutionary committee on
January is celebrated with a
ass rally organized by rebel
ctions (opposite). Three days
er, PLA soldiers march in
pport of the rebel groups and
e seizure of power from the
ovincial government (right).

Harbin, 7–16 February 1967

A group of "Little Red Guards"
admire the new four-volume
edition of *The Selected Works of
Mao Zedong* and the reprinted
Quotations from Mao Zedong.
The boys had walked from Baoqing
County, over 400 kilometers away,
and waited overnight in front
of a bookstore to buy the new
editions (opposite). A large crowd
gathers to cheer as rebel factions
and PLA soldiers smash and
burn the placard of the Harbin
municipal government in Red
Guard Square (right).

Two weeks after seizing power from the Harbin municipal government, rebels and the PLA continue to march in the streets to celebrate Mao and the revolution (below). Pan Fusheng and Fan Zhengmei (opposite, right and left), director and deputy director of the Heilongjiang revolutionary committee, fly from Harbin to Beijing to report on the situation in the province.

Harbin, 16 February–5 March 1967

Harbin, 27 April 1967

A huge crowd gathers in front of
the North Plaza Hotel to attend
the criticism of the former secretaries of the Heilongjiang Party
committee (opposite and below).
Wearing placards around their
necks, Li Fanwu, Wang Yilun, and
Ren Zhongyi (bottom, left to right)
are escorted to the stage.

163

In 1967, former Party officials became prize exhibits in the ongoing publicity campaign against "black gang elements." That spring, the blackest of all was Liu Shaoqi. Nominally still head of state, the public campaign against him began in April with an editorial in *People's Daily*, edited by Mao himself, which criticized the president as the "top Party person in power taking the capitalist road." Liu's home in Beijing was searched, and his wife was humiliated before a crowd of thousands of Red Guards at Qinghua University in Beijing by being forced to mount the stage wearing high heels, a sexy silk dress, and a necklace of ping-pong balls.

All over China, rallies were held condemning the once-revered leader. The campaign would reach a boiling point on 18 July, when the seventy-year-old Liu and his wife were roughly handled and made to bow for two hours during a criticism session inside Zhongnanhai, the leadership compound. After another criticism session a few weeks later, Liu Shaoqi was stripped of his duties.

For the next year he would be held in house arrest. When the Party finally officially ratified his overthrow the following summer as a "renegade, traitor, and scab," the former head of state, suffering from pneumonia, was already bedridden, could no longer speak, and was being fed intravenously. In October 1969, he was removed to Kaifang, in Henan province, and housed in an unheated building. Refused hospitalization, he died on 12 November.

Forced to stand on chairs in front of the North Plaza Hotel, the seven secretaries of the Heilongjiang Party committee are denounced for "carrying out Liu Shaoqi's revisionist line."

Harbin, 27 April 1967

The seven provincial Party committee secretaries Li Fanwu, Wang Yilun, Chen Lei, Ren Zhongyi (present in both photographs), Li Jianbai, Li Rui, and Tan Yunhe (left to right), are denounced by Red Guards in front of the North Plaza Hotel. Each wears a placard with his name crossed out and a description of his alleged crime.

Harbin, 27 April 1967

Li Fanwu

Wang Yilun

Chen Lei

Harbin, 27 April 1967

Two rebel factions fight for control of a broadcasting bus in front of the Heilongjiang revolutionary committee headquarters.

Harbin, 5 June 1967

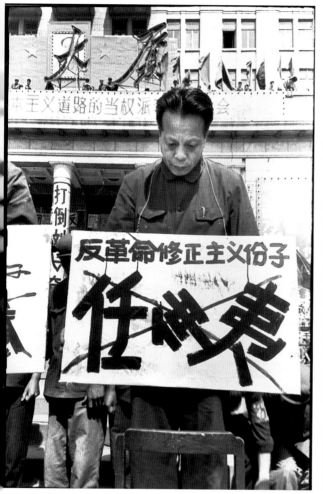

Ren Zhongyi

Li Jianbai

Li Rui

Tan Yunhe

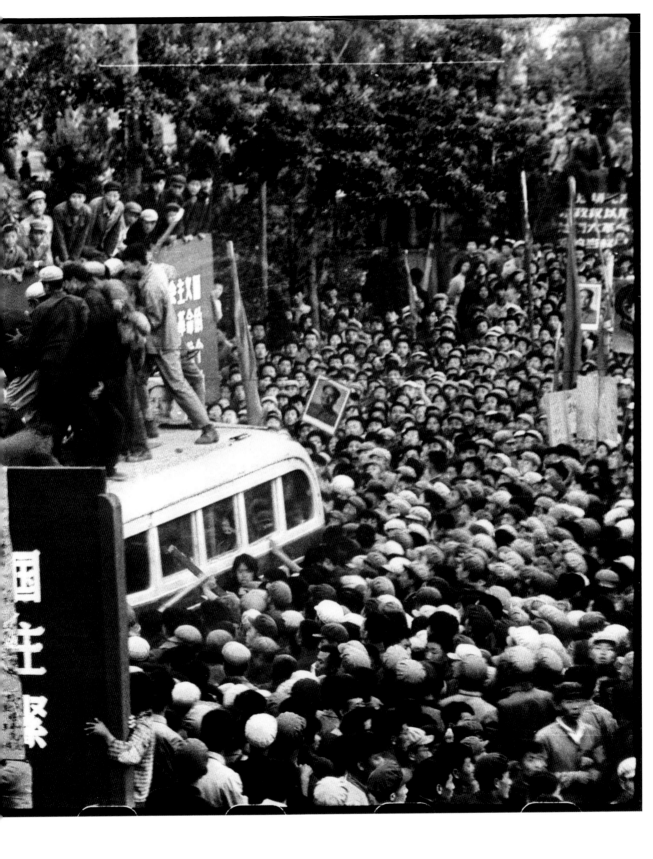

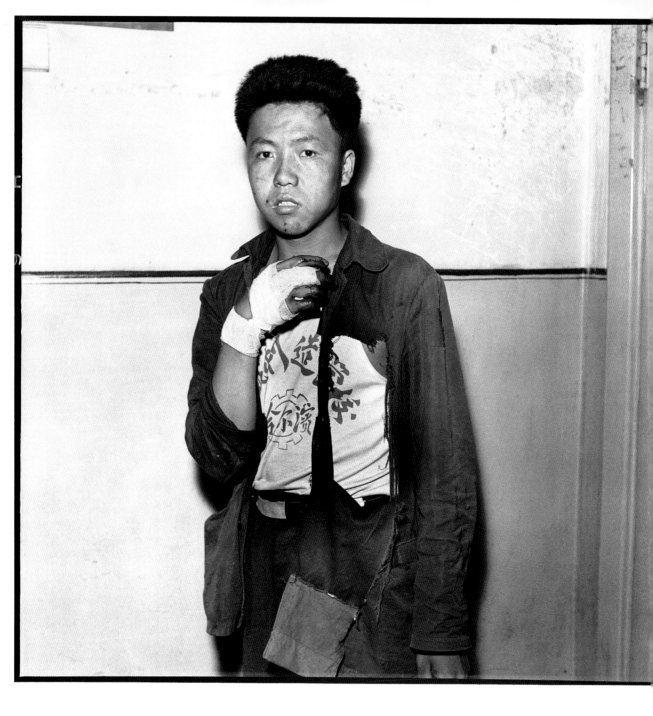

Harbin, 9 June 1967

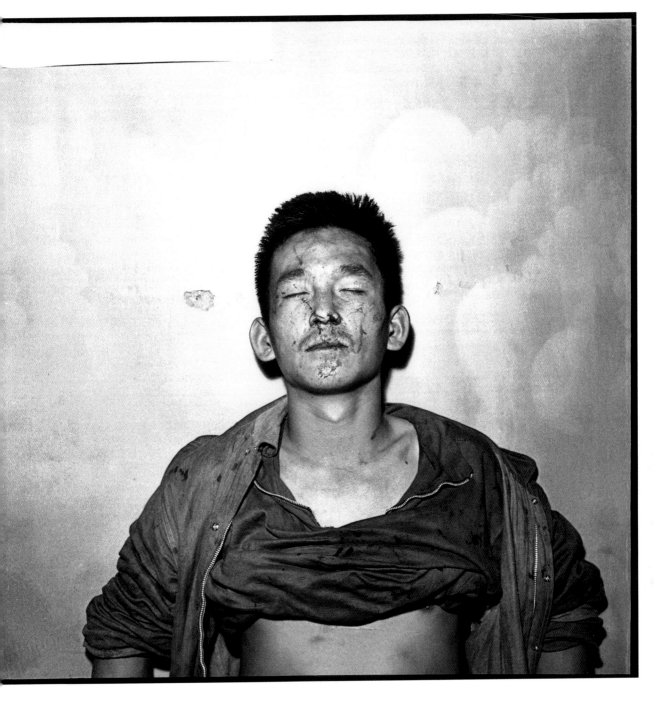

hts between rebel factions often
alated into combat, leading to
ury and even death. These
victims were photographed
r days after the clash over
control of a broadcasting bus,
ich injured scores and killed
veral, including the fatally
unded young man on the right.

Harbin, 17 June 1967

the evening following China's
st successful hydrogen-bomb
st, crowds flock to the street in
  outpouring of national pride.
e homemade sign reads,
armly cheer our first successful
bomb explosion."

China had conducted its first successful test of an atomic bomb in October 1964, in the early days of the Socialist Education Movement. Developed without the Soviet Union's assistance — a point that would lead to further deterioration of Sino-Soviet relations — it was code-named "596," referring to June 1959, when Soviet Premier Nikita Khrushchev had reversed the decision to provide the Chinese government with a prototype.

Three years later, despite the intervening chaos of the Cultural Revolution, Chinese scientists had constructed the nation's first hydrogen bomb. Shrouded in secrecy, the program had been carefully insulated by Mao from the general disorder. On one occasion Red Guard units, including the Chairman's own nephew Mao Yuanxin, threatened to storm a top-secret plant in Liaoning province in northeastern China where the research was taking place and were swiftly turned away by force. The need to control access to the bomb revealed the perils of revolutionary zeal and Mao's earlier invocation to "trust the masses."

In the summer of 1967, as conflict between rival rebel groups became increasingly ferocious, and the role of the army greatly expanded with the ascent of Lin Biao, the detonation of the hydrogen bomb on 17 June was one explosion all Chinese could celebrate.

Harbin, 28 June 1967

The Harbin Construction Institute
is destroyed following a battle
between rebel factions. Only
softcover books are left behind
on the library floor (above),
because all hardcover books had
been used by the rival groups as
projectile weapons.

Bayan county, Heilongjiang province, 8 July 1967

Red Guards across the
...ntry, fishermen along the upper
...ghua River on the outskirts
...Harbin eagerly demonstrate
...r devotion to Mao, criticizing
..."...Shaoqi's revisionist line" with
...anner and portraits of Mao.

Harbin, 16 July 1967

People in the Songhua River commemorate the one-year anniversary of Mao's swim in the Yangtze, which marked his return to power at the outbreak of the Cultural Revolution.

祝毛主席万寿无疆！

Heilongjiang province, July 1967

Elementary schoolchildren in Hulan county read the Little Red Book on their way to a study session of Mao's writings. The boy's sash reads, "It is right to rebel" (23 July, opposite). In a textile mill in Jiamusi City, a placard reminds workers to "Learn, carry out, propagandize, and protect Chairman Mao's supreme instruction. It is right to rebel" (25 July, bottom right). At the Harbin Power Equipment Factory, a young boy is the showpiece of the First Provincial Conference of Learning and Applying Mao Zedong Thought (28 July, right).

PLA member Zhang Chunyu addresses a crowd gathered in front of the North Plaza Hotel to commemorate the one-year anniversary of Mao Zedong's "Bombard the Headquarters" big character poster, which precipitated the Chairman's attack on the Party establishment at the start of the Cultural Revolution. The banner reads, "Down with Liu Shaoqi and Deng Xiaoping" (below). Red Guards at Harbin's University of Industry write big character posters that read, "Upsurge Revolutionary Criticism" and "Criticize China's Nikita Khrushchev — Liu Shaoqi" (opposite).

Harbin, 5 August–4 September 1967

掀起革命大批判

毛泽东思想宣传栏
第六期
哈工大新曙光基础课合团4/9

Harbin, 4 September 1967

Red Guards hang big character posters at Harbin's University of Industry. The billboard reads, "Follow Chairman Mao's great strategy and grasp the direction of revolutionary struggle."

Poor and lower-middle peasants hold a meeting at the North Plaza Hotel. The banner above the speaker reads, "Criticize the old times and cherish the new society."

Harbin, 5 April 1968

Harbin, 5 April 1968

By 1968, Mao's revolutionary formula of "struggle—criticism—transformation" had given way to a new prescription: execution. On 5 April 1968 during *Qingming*, the traditional festival honoring dead ancestors, military police attached to Heilongjiang's revolutionary committee hauled away seven men and one woman. Six — including the woman and her lover, who had murdered her husband — were common criminals. The other two were considered "counterrevolutionaries." Technicians at the Harbin Electric Meter Factory, they had been found guilty of publishing a flyer entitled "Looking Northward." Interpreted by the provincial revolutionary committee as a reference to China's neighbor to the North, the Soviet Union, and therefore promoting Soviet-style revisionism, they were both sentenced to death.

After the sentence was pronounced, one of the condemned counterrevolutionaries, named Wu Bingyuan, raised his head and shouted, "This world is too dark." Then he closed his eyes and never reopened them. With their hands tied behind their backs and placards hung around their necks advertising their alleged crimes, the eight condemned prisoners were loaded onto flatbed trucks and paraded through the lined streets of Harbin, then driven to a dusty plot of land adjoining the Huang Shan Cemetery on the northern outskirts of the city. There, Wu and the other seven were marched a short distance, made to kneel in a line, and shot.

Following a public trial, seven men and one woman are transported in open trucks from Harbin to Huang Shan Cemetery on the city outskirts. Amid the common criminals and "counterrevolutionaries" are two lovers, Cui Fengyuan (left) and Guan Jinxian (right), who conspired to murder the woman's husband.

Harbin and outskirts, 5 April 1968

er being paraded through the
owd-lined streets of Harbin
pposite), the condemned are
ven to the outskirts of the city.
e "counterrevolutionaries" Wu
ngyan (with his eyes closed)
d Wang Yongzeng bear placards
th their names and crimes
elow).

Outskirts of Harbin, 5 April 1968

The accused Li Wenye, Zhang Liangfu, Cui Fengyun, Guan Jingxian, Cheng Jinhai, Sun Fengwen, Wang Yongzeng, and Wu Bingyuan (left to right) are made to stand in line with their backs to the crowd that has gathered to watch the sentence being carried out.

The eight criminals and counter-revolutionaries are forced to kneel on the ground. In the moment before their execution, a guard attempts to separate the two condemned lovers Cui Fengyuan and Guan Jinxian (left).

Outskirts of Harbin, 5 April 1968

Outskirts of Harbin, 5 April 1968

伟大领袖毛主席同他的亲密战友林彪同志，在天安门城楼上检阅游行队伍。

首都国庆摄影报道组摄（新华社传真照片）

毛主席最新指示

广大干部下放劳动，这对干部是一种重新学习的极好机会，除老弱病残者外都应这样做。在职干部也应分批下放劳动。

黑龙江日报

黑龙江省革命委员会
机关报
1968年10月5日
星期六
第627号
夏历戊申年八月十四
（今日六版）

IV

In 1968, the political winds that would bring about my own downfall in the Cultural Revolution shifted. This was the era when ultraleftist forces — such as Vice-Chairman Lin Biao and Mao's wife, Jiang Qing — held sway in the Party. Newly reorganized, the Central Committee had been purged of all moderate elements. Liu Shaoqi and Deng Xiaoping were now condemned as a "bourgeois headquarters." The Red Guards had left behind a wake of infighting, school closures, and work stoppages — utter chaos. Now, under Mao's national "three-in-one" combination policy, teams of rebel leaders, veteran cadres, and PLA representatives throughout the country took power of the new revolutionary committees and reasserted Party control.

The head of Heilongjiang's provincial revolutionary committee, the province's new number-one man, Pan Fusheng, was determined to implement an ultraleftist line. He dispatched five cadres to the *Heilongjiang Daily*. The standing commission of the revolutionary committee at the paper, to which I belonged, was expanded from six to nine members, and one of the newest members was an appointee of the provincial revolutionary committee, a cadre by the name of Nie Gang.

I wasn't against the "three-in-one" policy, but I had some reservations. The newspaper was running just fine, I thought — and these "outside cadres" were untrained newsmen who had little to offer. "The provincial revolutionary committee doesn't need to send anyone else to the paper," I said during a meeting of the standing commission. "We can control the fate of our own newspaper."

Nie took notes — notes that would eventually be my undoing. In April, several student rebels and cadres, seeking to gain a foothold at the paper, seized on these remarks and began criticizing other commission members who had sided with me as "attacking the provincial revolutionary committee" — meaning the Party. No one yet mentioned me by name, but that was a standard tactic during the Cultural Revolution, to "point at the locust tree in order to revile the mulberry," and I knew it was only a matter of time before they got to me, too.

•

During the Cultural Revolution, photojournalists were not supposed to make so-called negative images — that is, of all the denunciations and torment of the time — and several different orders were given by the propaganda department of the provincial revolutionary committee, as well as the Red Guard organizations at the universities, for photographers to surrender their negatives. Most followed this order, and in the end their negatives were all set on fire and destroyed.

I usually processed all my film myself. Afterward I would cut out some of the negatives, all those images "beyond the assignment"— the condemnations and the

Front page of the *Heilongjiang Daily*, 5 October 1968. The photo caption reads, "Great Leader Chairman Mao and his close comrade in arms Lin Biao review the National Day parade at Tiananmen Gate." The headline reads, "The latest instruction of Chairman Mao," and the box below, "Cadres should go to the countryside to work. This is a very good opportunity for reeducation. All except the old or sick should go. Cadres who occupy official positions should also take turns to go to the countryside."

executions. These "negative" negatives I put into small paper pouches, then hid them away in a drawer in my office. The drawer had hidden slots I had designed myself. I rarely showed these images to my colleagues, but, of course, they'd seen me taking the pictures, and sometimes they also saw the negatives in the darkroom when I was processing them or when they were laid out on the drying cabinet.

In the fall of 1968, I was finally attacked by name. It happened when I returned to work after National Day on 1 October. The halls were covered with big character posters — and they were all about me: "Down with Li Zhensheng! Destroy the black underground headquarters!"

After that, more big character posters appeared, and I was suspended from the standing commission. The Red Guards of the opposing camp started an investigation. They went to my hometown in Shandong province, my high school in Dalian, and my film school in Changchun, searching for incriminating material in my family background, my school life, and my political dossier.

Li on the bank of the Songhua River in Harbin on the second anniversary of Mao's historic swim in the Yangtze. In the background is the Big Floods Memorial, built following the devastating floods in the summer of 1958 (photograph by Wang Zhili). 16 July 1968

Luckily, I had already transferred my negatives from the paper to my home. Six months after we were married, Yingxia and I had finally found a place to live together. It was twelve square meters big and far from the newspaper. Actually it was part of a Russian-style villa that had formerly belonged to a veteran cadre. After he was denounced for living too lavishly, it was divided among many families. There was no heat or gas or sewage system, and everyone shared a single makeshift toilet with wooden walls and a pit in the ground.

I cut a book-size hole in the floor under the desk Yingxia and I had bought with our marriage coupon. The floor was made of good quality wood, two layers thick, and it took me several days to saw through it. It had to be done very discreetly. Yingxia stood by the window, and whenever somebody approached on their way to bathroom, she signaled me to stop. I cut the wood at an angle so it would neatly fit back in, and attached a piece of string to the piece to be able to open it. Because we didn't have any plastic, I wrapped the bundles of negatives in oil cloth. I hid everything under the floor — the negatives along with some incriminating coins and stamps — then closed the hole and put the desk back in its place.

Soon after, on 30 October 1968, my son was born. Expressing my refusal to be cowed by the attacks against me, I named him Xiaohan — "laughing at the cold."

On the evening of 26 December 1968, Mao Zedong's seventy-fifth birthday, student rebels organized a criticism session exclusively for me. I was put onstage, made to bow, and criticized for over six hours continuously in front of more than three hundred of my colleagues. I was accused of wanting to dominate the paper, of attempting to create my own independent "kingdom," and of opposing the provincial revolutionary committee. This last accusation was very serious; Heilongjiang had been the first province in the country to establish a revolutionary committee, and an editorial in the *People's Daily* had called it the "first ray of the new morning light in northeastern China."

My crime was opposing the light.

The criticism was conducted by a young instructor from Harbin Teacher's College, Chen Yanzheng. Chen had a sharp, high-pitched voice and was a good orator. He had come to the newspaper as a Red Guard, but along with some others — such as the cadre Nie who quietly maneuvered behind the scenes — he found life at the newspaper agreeable and had no wish to leave. Chen, who had been granted access to my file at the newspaper, revealed the contents of my diaries and correspondence, how, after missing my chance to join the Xinhua News Agency in Beijing, I had written, "I'm not going to die in Heilongjiang." Apparently, someone had read it and made a report. Now the rebels interrogated me: "We have thirty-two million people living in Heilongjiang province," they said. "They have been living here for centuries. How come you can't live here and die here?"

But they didn't want to hear the story behind it. They held up photographs of Yingxia and me, especially those where I looked chic. All of it was used against me. Because I was not born in a bourgeois family, the rebel cadres called me a "newly born bourgeois."

One by one, all of my "crimes" were brought to light: my brush with the school authorities back at the Changchun Film School; my diaries from the "four cleanups," where I had expressed some sympathy for the heroine of a denounced film, *Early Spring*. My former secretary denounced me, too, revealing the episode of the reference letter for the former rightist's wife. You couldn't go against it. When another of my former secretaries, a woman named Lin Xianjuan, refused to make any criticism against me, she was brought onto the stage and denounced too.

My disagreement with the outside cadres at the paper was known to everyone, but my colleagues didn't know about the other incidents, and it made them angry. One Red Guard, a young and very tall student from Harbin Teachers College, Wang Wensheng, even called me a foreign agent! At that time, it was illegal to send any newspapers abroad. But Wang had discovered that I had used local papers to wrap up stamps I had sent to my stamp-trading partners in Indonesia and Japan when I

Li (front row, far right) with co-members of the *Heilongjiang Daily* revolutionary committee posing for a group picture in front of the newspaper building in Harbin (photograph by Wan Jyao). 7 May 1968

205

was in middle school. He came up to me and ripped the Mao badge off my coat. "You are a foreign agent, a newly born bourgeois. You are not entitled to this!"

An even more despicable accusation came from Chen. "We accuse Li Zhensheng of sexual assault!" he told the assembly in a shocked voice. "Under the pretext of showing photographs to a very virtuous female Red Guard, he made his assault!" Chen didn't mention the name of the "victim," but I knew very well what he was talking about. There were three female Red Guards at the paper, and at

Li's son, Xiaohan, in the family home in Harbin sitting at the desk under which Li cut a hole in 1968 to hide his negatives.
19 February 1973

the time one of them, Feng, actually lived in a small room close to the photography lab. Feng had a friend, another female Red Guard named Ma, who often came by to visit. Ma studied fine arts at Harbin Teacher's College. Once she asked to see my work, and as I opened the cabinet to retrieve some photographs, my arm brushed her cheek. I apologized, but as it happened, her boyfriend was another member of the standing commission. He knew, as did Ma, that the accusation was ludicrous, but agreed to let cadres Nie and Chen use the incident if they promised not to mention Ma by name.

When I heard the allegation, I was furious. Even though I was supposed to remain bowing, showing humility, I raised my head and yelled out her name. "Let Ma come up here herself!" I challenged them. "Let me confront her — and then we'll find out the truth about it!" Of course, Chen couldn't let that happen; the whole scheme would unravel. So instead he just shouted, "The accused has no right to ask questions!" Later, he turned to the crowd. "In four days, it will be a new year," he said. Then he shouted a slogan that for the rest of my life I will never forget: "Down with Li Zhensheng so we can embrace a glorious 1969!" "What? The new year won't come if Li Zhensheng isn't overthrown?" I thought to myself.

The criticism lasted until the middle of the night. Then a team led by the tall Red Guard, Wang Wensheng, went to my apartment to find more evidence against me. At home, the only heat we had came from a coal-burning stove. It was freezing outside, and with the doors thrown open the room quickly became icy. Wang forced me to open all my drawers and cabinets while the baby cried in Yingxia's arms. Having discovered some personal photographs of the two of us, he scornfully held them up to show his comrades. "Just look at these petty bourgeois," he sneered.

The negatives were under the floor. I didn't think Wang would find them — but even so, as he and his cohorts rifled through our belongings, I stood in front of the desk covering the hole. They confiscated several stamp albums and many letters and photographs in order to "launch a complete political investigation." But when Wang grabbed a bundle of our love letters, Yingxia got upset and told him to leave them alone. "A Communist Party member has nothing to hide," he replied smugly.

I was concerned for Yingxia. We didn't have a phone, so I couldn't call to warn her beforehand. And she had given birth less than two months before. Some people in China believe that if a woman who has just had a baby is surprised, she will later suffer from menstrual disorders or infertility. So I wanted to keep Yingxia calm. I wanted to be strong for her. But after six hours of being condemned, I was so tired myself that it was she who supported me. After the Red Guards left, I fell flat on the bed. She held back her own tears and tried to comfort me. "Please be strong," she urged. "We didn't do anything wrong."

My crimes were not serious enough for the paper to dismiss me, but from that day forward I was no longer permitted to take photographs. My cameras were taken away, and I wasn't allowed to return to my office. Instead, they assigned me to clip articles from the newspaper in the Office of Comprehensive Information.

The head of the Office of Comprehensive Information was none other than the same tall Red Guard who had led the search of my house, Wang Wensheng, and relations between us were very bad. He constantly bossed me around and tried to provoke me. One day, when I was cutting out some articles and the two of us were alone in the room, he said to me: "Li Zhensheng, why didn't you admit that you sexually assaulted Ma, such a good comrade?"

"Ma is upstairs right now," I shot back. "Tell her to come down and let's ask her a few questions."

i drying his prints in the
hotography lab of the
Heilongjiang Daily in Harbin
photograph by Wan Jiyao).
5 September 1968

"Do we really need to continue harassing her?" he asked.

"Fine. Have it your way. Then I'll admit it to you. But first we need to open the door so I can go into the corridor and shout it. That way everyone can hear: 'I raped Ma!'"

There were offices on both sides of the corridor and Wang, who knew very well that they had cooked up this story, didn't want everyone to hear about it. I was already married, but Ma, the standing commission member's girlfriend, would be disgraced. "How dare you say that," he screamed. "Even now, you are verbally assaulting her!" Then, although he was several years younger than me, he slapped me in the face — on my left cheek. It was the only time in my life that anyone other than my father ever hit me, and at that moment I'm sure I could have really hurt him. But I knew if I hit him back, it would mean my future. So I gritted my teeth and told him, "Remember this day! Remember this slap!"

After that incident, Wang always tried to avoid me; but as it happened, I saw him again thirty years later. I had gone to the *Heilongjiang Daily* for a visit, and suddenly, while talking to some colleagues, there he was. Wang stood there blinking; he couldn't believe his eyes. When I offered my hand, he flinched. He thought I was going to hit him back! — and his face turned red just as if I had.

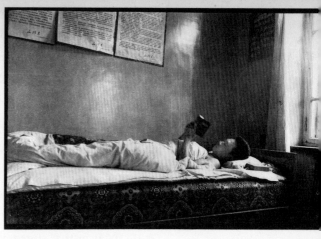

Li reads Mao's works while on assignment for the *Heilongjiang Daily* at Lalin Airforce base in Wuchang county (photographed with a self-timer). 5 July 1969

•

On 6 September 1969, together with twenty-six others, including my wife, I was sent to the Liuhe May 7th Cadre School in the countryside. These schools of "rectification," created by Mao two years earlier through the famous 7 May directive, were set up all over China and placed under the authority of the provincial revolutionary committees. Liuhe, in a remote area in Qingan County, halfway between Harbin and the Soviet border, was famous for being the very first.

During the "four cleanups" we had gone to the countryside to lead, to mobilize. We attended the May 7th School to be reformed. This was to be accomplished through work, hard work, every day. We cut grass, chopped wood, cleared the forest, built roads. I was not supposed to take pictures, but I had secretly brought two cameras with me, a Soviet-made Zorki 35 mm and a Chinese-made Shanghai 4 twin-lens medium-format camera. I only managed to take a few pastoral images here and there, and I was especially careful about protecting my eyes and fingers, as many people lost fingers cutting wood.

In some ways, it was a return to the old boarding-school days: thirty to forty people all huddled together on a large makeshift bed. I often slept with my clothes on because we would sometimes be woken up in the middle of the night to go out on marches. This was considered militia training, but it was actually a form of torture. For meals we were given steamed bread made of corn, or rice full of sand, and watery turnip soup. The shredded turnips were at the bottom of the pot, but you weren't allowed to stir it. Once, when the former president of the Heilongjiang People's High Court tried, he was criticized for following an "anti-Mao line." The remaining shredded turnips were given to the pigs.

It is difficult to imagine the hardship we went through — especially the women. In the wintertime, even if they were menstruating or pregnant, they still had to break the ice, stand in the freezing water up to their waists, and then reach down to cut the thatch.

My first job was with the school construction company, making prefabricated boards for the houses of the school. We made these boards by mixing ground wood chips with plaster, then pouring the mix into a wooden frame, covering it, and pushing it on a cart along two rails into a kiln, where it was baked until hard. Hot air blew into the kiln in a pit beneath the rails; we had to walk between the rails and pay attention not to fall in. We had to tie our sleeves and trousers to protect ourselves from dust and ash. It felt like a boiler room in there, and all day long we shuttled between the heat and the frigid cold outside. Conditions were unbearable. Once I saw a man killed when he was hit in the head with a board. He died in an instant. His body was thrown carelessly into a ditch and buried.

After the hard manual labor, at night we all had to study Mao's works, and to participate in discussions and analyze our world outlook in relation to Mao Zedong Thought. Mao touched every aspect of our lives. Once an old lady fell between the rails. After she was taken out, instead of being brought to the clinic, she was forced to analyze why she had fallen. It was said that her error was that she didn't "step on Mao's line." On another occasion, the former president of the Heilongjiang People's High Court leaned a spade against a wall, and it toppled over. He had been in Yanan with Mao in the early 1940s. Now he was asked to analyze why his spade had fallen.

Married couples were not allowed to live together at the school, and Yingxia was in a different company from mine. Sometimes I could see her while I was working, and we would catch each other's eye and just nod. There was a small room where every couple could stay together one night a month. On those nights, Yingxia often cried. We had left our son, Xiaohan, with his grandmother in Shandong province. He was less than a year

Li calls a friend from his office in Harbin to bid farewell before his departure for the Liuhe May 7th Cadre School in the country-side (photographed with a self-timer). 1 September 1969

old and hadn't even finished breastfeeding. We missed him terribly, but we couldn't let our feelings show. Physically, spiritually, and mentally we were suffering, but all the time we had to act as if, even though we were separated from each other and our son, we were happy to be there. We had suffered during the famine. We suffered again during the "four cleanups" when I was first sent down to the country-side — but even though we were hungry then, we knew that after a year or so we would be able to return to our homes. At the May 7th School there was no such guarantee.

·

The only news from the outside world at the school came from the loudspeaker. I listened closely, knowing that any shift in the political wind could change our fate. That's why, when the loudspeaker announced the overthrow of Pan Fusheng, the head of Heilongjiang's provincial revolutionary committee, in May 1971, I got very excited. Since Heilongjiang had been the first province in the country to establish a revolutionary committee, the overthrow of its first director signaled a major shift in the policy of the Central Committee and of Mao.

Pan's departure threw the May 7th School into a state of confusion. Who was in charge? The school was actually run by people who had been criticized themselves but who were considered "trusted cadres." But with Pan gone, whom would they report to? Eventually, people just started to leave. They would register with school personnel, saying, "my mother is sick," or "my wife is going to give birth," and no one prevented their going. Giving the excuse that my father was seriously ill and that we needed to see after our son, in August Yingxia and I left, too. We hitched a ride on a tractor to the local train station and headed home.

After visiting Xiaohan in Shandong, we returned to Harbin. That's when, before the news was officially disclosed, a friend told me all about the momentous event: "Baldhead Lin is dead!" he cried when we were safely alone. Lin Biao, Mao's would-be successor, he told me, had betrayed the Chairman and was killed when his escape plane crashed in Mongolia on its way to the Soviet Union.

I hadn't liked Lin from the start. He had fought courageously against Chiang Kai-shek in the 1940s, but it was Lin who had implemented the ultraleftist line, the "four greats," the Little Red Book, Lin who represented the very forces in control of the May 7th Schools. Not only that, but he was also ugly — a real monkey face. In the family house in Shandong province we had a photograph of Lin and Mao on the wall. I remember my mother once frowning at the picture. "Look at him," she said pointing at Lin. "He's not like Mao — he's more like his stable boy." Lin's death brought about significant political change; some ultraleftist policies were abandoned, and many people started to doubt the Cultural Revolution and to publicly raise questions addressing some of the wrongdoing of the previous years.

I felt that I had been mistreated, that I had merely been the victim in a power struggle among rebel factions that had nothing to do with revolution. So instead of returning to the May 7th Cadre School, as I should have, I spent the days making contact with former allies, trying to make our return permanent. With the help of two friends named Bai and Liu, I wrote some big characters and posted them on a wall near the provincial revolutionary committee. They read, "Those in power at the *Heilongjiang Daily* have been implementing a capitalist line — suppressing true revolutionaries and expelling all those not in agreement with them. The *Heilongjiang Daily* must totally implement the Party's new policy toward intellectuals!" Signed, "The Staff of the *Heilongjiang Daily*."

Liu was a friend from film school, also a photographer, whom I had helped get a job at the Agricultural Exhibition Hall. Bai was a painter who lived in his dorm. I have a very distinctive calligraphy, and I didn't want anyone at the paper to recognize me as the author, so I had Bai paint the characters for me. Then we gathered the sheets of paper and glue and prepared to paste them up. But Liu and Bai were heavy drinkers. That night, before we left, we had a meal, and the two of them drank grain alcohol until they got very drunk. The next evening, we had another meal, more drinks, and again Liu and Bai got drunk. Finally, on the third night, I pleaded with them not to drink anything until after we hung the banner, and we finally managed to put it up.

My big characters created an immediate sensation. The provincial revolutionary committee took it very seriously and telephoned the *Heilongjiang Daily*. Many people in positions of power at the paper, already threatened by the new political climate, grew very nervous. After Pan Fusheng's overthrow, in accordance with the new national policy, the standing commission was abolished, the former editor in chief Zhao Yang was brought back, and at top-level meetings, commission members, rather than accusing the other side and condemning enemies, made self-criticisms.

These meetings were called "climbing the slope," referring to Mao's instruction for all of China to strive to "unite for a greater victory," and in February 1972 a meeting of all the rebel factions took place. Representing the Red Rebel League and the staff, I made an emotional self-criticism. I admitted that my group had attacked the weaknesses of the other side in order to prove we were more revolutionary. There is a famous Chinese poem that says, "With a leaf in front of your eyes, you can't see the Tai mountains." For my self-criticism, I updated it. "Divided into different factions which blocked our eyesight," I said, "we were blind to the main direction." The room, full of former allies and enemies alike, filled with cheers.

uring his reeducation at the
iuhe May 7th Cadre School in
ingan county, Li, who had
ecretely managed to take two
ameras with him, was only
ole to make a few landscape
hotographs "out of admi-
ation for nature's vitality."
 December 1970 (right) and
January 1971 (far right)

Li in the woods of Qingan county at the Liuhe May 7th Cadre School, where he spent two years being reeducated (photographed with a self-timer). 15 February 1970

After the meeting, my old editor Zhao Yang invited me back to work. Zhang Ge, the tall photographer who had been the head of the photo team, had retired, and I was named to lead the team in his place. After more than two years in the countryside, I was officially sent home.

I don't think it hit me for months — not until that spring, when I was one of two photographers from the paper assigned to cover the state visit of Prince Sihanouk of Cambodia. This was my first big assignment after "reeducation," and I accompanied the prince the entire time he was in Harbin. The first day, riding in a Red Flag limousine in his motorcade, the sides of the road thronged with flag-waving crowds, it suddenly struck me: after having experienced so much — the condemnation, the search of my apartment, the long, freezing marches and the labor at the May 7th Cadre School — I had survived. I was still here, still standing.

1968–1972

By 1968, the bloodletting of the previous years had left power firmly in the hands of Mao and a small coterie including Lin Biao and Mao's wife, Jiang Qing. With former president Liu Shaoqi purged, and all of China's twenty-nine provinces now in the hands of the new provincial revolutionary committees, the Red Guards, whose anarchic impulses had incited civil warfare, were dissolved, their purpose fulfilled.

To redirect the destructive energies of the student rebels who had left school to make revolution, and to counteract growing unemployment in the cities, the Chairman launched a new mass movement in the countryside. Named after a letter Mao had written to Lin Biao on 7 May 1966 about work-study among the peasants, the May 7th Cadre School program was a sprawling gulag system that combined hard manual labor with assiduous study of Mao's writings. Over the next four years, millions of Party cadres purged in the campaign to "cleanse class ranks" attended May 7th Schools throughout rural China. Joined by an additional five million "educated youth" sent to live among poor peasants for reeducation, this relocated multitude came to be known as the "sent down" generation.

Over the following years, under a banner of "continuing revolution while increasing production," Mao steered the Cultural Revolution into a new phase. The focus of state-sponsored propaganda shifted toward positive reinforcement of prescribed values, stressing the inherent goodness of the communist revolution and the virtues of conformity and dedication to Mao. Devotees were shown as vigorous and loyal, beaming with health and happiness. Children, natural models of these traits, often became the front-line troops in the manufacture of good news, ideal symbols of the nation's projected rebirth after years of struggle. The message was simple: as Premier Zhou Enlai had put it several years earlier: "All that accords with Mao Zedong Thought is right. All that does not is wrong."

But behind the elderly leader hovered the two supporting architects of the cataclysm: Lin Biao, who controlled the army, and Jiang Qing and her group of Shanghai radicals, soon to become infamous as the "Gang of Four." With all moderate voices silenced and no one else left to fight, Lin and Jiang, in keeping with Mao's dictum of perpetual revolution, began a lethal competition for Mao's favor and the future leadership of China.

Harbin, Heilongjiang province, 16 April 1968

During a three-week-long
Conference of Learning and
Applying Mao Zedong Thought,
Wang Guoxiang, a model PLA
soldier, shares his experiences
from a meeting in Xinfa commune
just outside Harbin, where the
audience pinned some 170 Mao
badges on his cap and uniform to
express their admiration.

Kang Wenjie, a five-year-old prodigy, performs the "loyalty dance" at Harbin's Red Guard Stadium for representatives of the Conference on Learning and Applying Mao Zedong Thought.

Harbin, 28 April 1968

Hundreds of thousands gather in
front of the North Plaza Hotel
carrying homemade portraits of Mao
in a show of loyalty and support.

Harbin, 21 June 1968

A Mao Zedong Thought propaganda team sings Mao's quotations in Taiping commune (11 July, below left). Swimmers prepare to plunge into the Songhua River to commemorate the second anniversary of Mao's swim in the Yangtze (16 July, below right and bottom left). Workers in the Harbin Arts and Crafts Factory make Mao plaques (18 July, bottom right). Writers and artists march through Wuchang county on their way to participate in manual labor (18 August, opposite).

Harbin, September–October 1968

Military-hospital patients make their morning pledge of loyalty to Mao's picture (5 September, below). On 1 October, Harbin celebrates National Day with fireworks along the Songhua River, parades of schoolgirls and the PLA, and marchers carrying a statue of Mao on a float adorned with sunflowers symbolizing the Chinese people following Mao the way flowers follow the sun (clockwise from below right).

Harbin and Shangzhi county, 6–11 October 1968

A Mao Zedong Thought propaganda team spreads Mao's instructions at the University of Industry in Harbin (opposite), while peasants in the countryside gather to read "A letter to peasants from the Central Committee of the Chinese Communist Party" published in the *Heilongjiang Daily* (above).

Harbin, 14 October 1968

Returning from the National Day
celebration in Beijing, Heilongjiang's
revolutionary committee delegation
is greeted at Harbin's railway station
with gifts of wax mangos, emulating
the seven real mangos given to
Mao by a delegation from Pakistan
the previous August. Mao presented
these mangos to seven worker-
peasant propaganda teams responsible for quelling the factional
fighting of the Red Guards.
The bestowal of mangos came to
symbolize Mao's trust in the
workers after the dissolution of
the Red Guards.

As China lurched toward stability, the terror continued. With the first ranks of the denounced already dead or dispatched to China's remote regions, rebel forces often took aim at the relatives they left behind. Guilt in the Cultural Revolution, like in the anti-rightist campaign of the 1950s before it, was hereditary. Sons and daughters of alleged counterrevolutionaries and revisionists — like the sons and daughters of the accused capitalists and rightists before them — were tainted by their parents' crimes and frequently shared their fate.

A particularly infamous case in Harbin at the end of 1968 involved the son of the former first Party secretary of Heilongjiang. Preceding the outbreak of the Cultural Revolution, Ouyang Qin was the most powerful man in the province and therefore the number-one target of the Red Guards. Denounced, he was spared the full wrath of the guards when Premier Zhou Enlai, with whom he had been friendly since the 1920s when they both studied in France, had him transferred to a military hospital in Beijing for his protection in the summer of 1966. His son, however, would be less fortunate.

Ouyang Xiang's crime was writing an anonymous letter to the provincial revolutionary committee professing his father's total support of Mao. Deemed by Pan Fusheng a serious counterrevolutionary case needing to be cracked, within days Ouyang's handwriting was identified, and he was arrested. On 30 November 1968, a public rally was held in front of Harbin's North Plaza Hotel. Labeled a counterrevolutionary, Ouyang Xiang was made to wear a placard around his neck detailing his crime and the date of his letter. When he tried to shout, "Long live Chairman Mao," his mouth was stuffed with a dirty glove. Several days later he was pushed out of a third-story window of the office building where he was being held. The official report called his death a suicide.

Ouyang Xiang, son of the former first secretary of Heilongjiang's provincial Party committee, is dragged outside the North Plaza Hotel and persecuted for sending an unsigned letter to the provincial revolutionary committee defending his denounced father.

As he tries to shout in his defense, Ouyang Xiang's mouth is stuffed with a glove. The sign around his neck bears his name and the date of his offending letter.

Harbin, 30 November 1968

Harbin, 30 November 1968

Several days after this criticism
session in front of the North Plaza
Hotel, Ouyang Xiang would be
pushed out of a window on the
third floor of an office building by
a member of a rebel faction.
The official report would call his
death a suicide.

Red Guards in Harbin on Mao's 75th birthday (26 December 1968, below left) and PLA pilots and soldiers at Lalin Airforce base (19 July 1969, below right and bottom left) study the Little Red Book. During a screening of the documentary film *Chairman Mao, The Red Sun in Our Hearts*, students hail each of Mao's appearances (23 July, bottom right). Workers at the Mudanjiang Press pack the new one-volume edition of the *Selected Works of Mao Zedong* (10 August, opposite).

A central tenet of the May 7th
Cadre School program was that
manual labor could be an effective
means of erasing elitism and
reinstalling socialist values. Here,
May 7th "soldiers" thresh grain in
the northern part of Heilongjiang.

Xinsheng commune, Qingan county, 4 November 1969

The first May 7th Cadre School in China was established at the remote Liuhe farm, in Heilongjiang's Qingan county, 150 kilometers north of the capital, Harbin. Here, as at camps throughout the country, families were separated, with members living and sleeping together in segregated barracks. Days consisted of manual labor: farming, forest clearing, building construction. Nights were spent immersed in study of Mao Zedong Thought.

In contrast to the Socialist Education Movement of the mid-1960s when cadres from the cities typically spent a year living, eating, and working among the peasants, stays at the May 7th schools were indefinite. Largely isolated from the world beyond the camp, attendees, dubbed "May 7th soldiers," found themselves living in harsh environments with no reason to believe they would ever return to their homes.

But the death of Lin Biao, the program's leading proponent, in the fall of 1971 was to have a decisive impact on the fate of the schools. Worried that the Chairman had lost confidence in him, Lin was alleged to have plotted to assassinate Mao by blowing up his private train. When the supposed plot was revealed, Lin fled the country in an air-force Trident jet en route to the Soviet Union. For reasons still unknown, the plane never made it. It crashed in Mongolia on 13 September 1971, killing all aboard.

"Soldiers" from the Liuhe May 7th Cadre School pose for a group picture in front of a famed painting depicting Mao's trip to Anyuan in Hunan province. Mao had first achieved national prominence by his coordination of a miner's strike at Anyuan in 1922.

Qingan county, 15 December 1969

239

Qingan county, 18 December 1970

May 7th "soldiers" from the
Liuhe May 7th Cadre School pose
for a group picture in front of a
house they have just built.
Li, who took the photograph with
a self-timer, is in second row,
fifth from left.

Lin Biao's alleged betrayal of Mao and his subsequent death would shape China's trajectory for years to come. Its immediate impact was to loosen the stronghold of the May 7th Cadre Schools and the associated ultraleft policies. But perhaps its biggest effect was on Mao himself. Reportedly devastated by Lin's betrayal, the Chairman, now seventy-seven years old and in failing health, took to his bed for two months at his residence in Beijing.

But Mao would rouse himself one last time. Threatened by escalating skirmishes with Soviet troops near China's northern border at the Wusuli River, in a surprising reversal, he made several public overtures to the United States, including an invitation to the U.S. table-tennis team to visit China on a goodwill mission, even as American military forces continued to wage war in Southeast Asia. Following a few more rounds of "ping-pong diplomacy," U.S. Secretary of State Henry Kissinger secretly met his Chinese counterpart Zhou Enlai on January 1972 to arrange the meeting of the nations' two top leaders in Beijing the following month. Between these two events, the long-standing claim of the People's Republic of China for the United Nations' seat held by Taiwan was finally granted.

The historic first meeting between President Richard Nixon, the staunch anti-communist, and Mao, the lifelong revolutionary, took place on 18 February 1972, marking the end of China's period of "closed-door" isolation. Three months later, on the occasion of a state visit by deposed Cambodian Prince Sihanouk, Mao also decided to mend fences with another old nemesis, China's principal reformer and future leader Deng Xiaoping.

Harbin, 23 May 1972

Large crowds welcome the motorcade of Prince Norodom Sihanouk of Cambodia during his official visit to Harbin. After being deposed in a military coup in March 1970, the prince lived in exile in Beijing until returning to Cambodia in 1975.

Sino-Soviet relations were especially volatile in 1969 and the early 1970s, and skirmishes along the border were common, leading to armed militia patrols like this one near Rahoe on the Wusuli River, which marks the border at the northeastern tip of China.

Heilongjiang province, 23 September 1972

黑龙江日报

战无不胜的马克思主义、列宁主义、毛泽东思想万岁!

伟大的、光荣的、正确的中国共产党万岁!

一九七六年九月十日

伟大的领袖和导师毛泽东主席永垂不朽!

V.

After we returned from the May 7th Cadre School at the end of 1971, life was very different from the one we had known before we were sent down. The Red Guards were gone. Lin Biao was gone. The mass criticisms, the dunce caps, the placards — all of it was over. In 1966, if you merely accused someone of being conventional, they would get angry. Five years later, everyone was more relaxed, wanted to stay home, bring up children, make furniture. The worst of the red storm was over.

Yingxia and I quickly made up for lost time. First, we fetched our son Xiaohan from his grandparents' home in Shandong province. A toddler by then, he had no memory of us and was speaking with a thick Shandong accent — a real country boy. Then, two weeks before Mao met with President Richard Nixon in his Study of Chrysanthemum Fragrance in Beijing, our daughter was born on 6 February 1972. We named her Xiaobing — "laughing at the ice."

After the cold and lonely days of manual labor, I suddenly found myself with a family. We all lived in one room, the same one where I had hidden my negatives. The days of searches being over, I no longer had any reason to keep them hidden and had since put them away in a locked drawer. Like me, people were being restored to their former positions, including the previous tenant of our apartment, the veteran cadre who had been denounced for living too lavishly. Eventually the entirety of his villa was returned to him, so we had to leave. But we were very happy; we moved into a two-room apartment instead, and started our new life.

⚬

But while the political winds had changed, it was not necessarily true of people's hearts and minds. After the "climbing the slope" meeting at the paper, everyone became friendly again, but it was a facade. Resentments among old adversaries — even allies — lingered, sometimes carrying on among their children. Distrust and suspicion pervaded the Cultural Revolution until the end.

An example is what happened when I applied for membership to the Communist Party. I had made my first application when I was still in film school. At that time, every student wanted to become a member. It was a sign of being a progressive youth, and our motives were very pure. Only one of the 150 students at my school was a member, but I actually thought I had a good chance of being accepted. My brother was a revolutionary martyr, my father a model worker and a Party member, and I myself had joined the Young Pioneers in elementary school and the Communist Youth League in middle school. The Party authorities, however, decided that I focused too much on "personal fame and gain" and rejected me.

The front page of the *Heilongjiang Daily* on 10 September 1976 announces the death of Mao Zedong. The headline reads, "Eternal glory to the immortal great leader and teacher Chairman Mao."

Li with his wife, Yingxia, their son, Xiaohan, and daughter, Xiaobing, in their home in Harbin (photographed with a self-timer). 28 September 1972

When I began working at the *Heilongjiang Daily*, being a Communist Party member became a practical matter as well. The other four photographers at the paper were all older than me and they were all members, and the fact that I wasn't and couldn't attend official Party events, seriously affected my work. Even after becoming head of the team, I still had to assign other photographers to cover big Party functions like the provincial congress. On these occasions, some of the other photographers made jokes about me behind my back. I didn't find it funny; it was humiliating, a kind of political discrimination. That's why, after returning from the May 7th School, I applied for membership again.

At that time the Party made a very thorough inquiry of every applicant. They went to your hometown, your university, your place of work, met with your friends and colleagues, examined your file. So, for the second time in my life, I was investigated. That's when I discovered that the newest member of the photography team, Liu Hongshan, was leading the investigation. I had recruited Liu myself. He was a friend of one of the short photographers, my former ally from the Red Youth Fighting Team, Wan Jiyao, and worked in a Communications Section in Hulan county, on the outskirts of Harbin. He sometimes contributed photographs to the paper. In June 1972 he was about to be transferred to work in a commune broadcasting station and begged me to help him. I did. I gave him a job at the *Heilongjiang Daily* and arranged for his whole family to be relocated to Harbin. Now, he repaid my kindness by zealously prosecuting my investigation and secretly blocking my Party membership.

He found a pretext in a trip I made to my hometown to visit my parents in May 1973. This trip had special significance for me because I had arranged to meet my old

Indonesian stamp-trading partner from back in middle school, Zeng Qingrui. With my encouragement, Qingrui, an "overseas Chinese," had come to China in the early 1960s to study. After graduation he was assigned to teach in a middle school in Shandong province, about a hundred kilometers from my family home.

Both of us were very excited. Although we had corresponded since 1957, we had never met. Because we wouldn't recognize each other, I told him in advance what I would be wearing. To be conspicuous, I put on dark sunglasses, a peaked hat, and had a silver-colored camera bag on my shoulder — a very exotic outfit in China at that time. So when I stepped off the bus in this outfit, it caused quite a stir. I could have been a secret agent! Laughing, Qingrui spotted me, and we went back to his home. His wife took half a day off her job at the textile mill, cooked dumplings, and we all had a good time.

But having lived abroad, Qingrui and his wife were always viewed with suspicion and were routinely followed. Immediately after our meeting, the principal of Qingrui's school questioned him. What was all this about a mysterious rendezvous with a foreigner in sunglasses? If he and I really were such longtime friends, why couldn't he recognize me?

When I returned to the paper a few days later, I told my colleagues all about the meeting; I even showed them some pictures I'd taken. But alerted by the committee carrying out the inquiry for my Party membership, Liu went to Shandong province to investigate. He met with Qingrui's principal. He didn't tell him that the man in the sunglasses was me, his colleague. Instead, he merely noted down the accusation. Then, when he returned to the paper, he reported to the committee that, yes, Li Zhensheng's friend had participated in a "suspicious meeting with a guest from abroad." Liu's

Li (second from left) and other journalists pose with Prince Norodom Sihanouk and his wife, Queen Norodom Monineath (center), in front of Garden Village, Harbin's official residence for foreign dignitaries (photograph by Hu Wei). 26 May 1972

behavior reminded me of a fable in which a scholar named Dong Guo stops to help a wounded wolf and is almost eaten. In fact, I had an illustration of this fable and put it underneath the glass on my desk. When Liu saw it, he turned red. He knew it was meant for him. "You have no right to feel that way," he complained. "We had to follow the proper procedures."

"If I had followed the proper procedures," I told him, "you wouldn't be here."

My Party membership application was rejected.

•

Under the leadership of Premier Zhou Enlai and newly rehabilitated Vice-Premier Deng Xiaoping, in the early 1970s China quickly started to rebuild, but it was not the end of political movements. Set against the moderates like Zhou and Deng stood the Shanghai group who wanted the revolution to go on forever: Mao's wife, Jiang Qing, and the other three radicals, Zhang Chunqiao, Yao Wenyuan, and Wang Hongwen — the Gang of Four. In late 1973, a new campaign was launched to criticize Lin Biao and Confucius as reactionary feudalists. But few people became very passionate about it. Most, I think, saw it for what it was: a calculated attempt on the part of Jiang Qing to topple Zhou Enlai. But while Zhou was very popular, Jiang was not. I dare say not a single person in China liked her — not even Mao.

In addition to being vengeful and power-hungry, Mao's wife was also quite stupid. For example, for Nixon's visit she wanted the Americans to see the Chinese using their own products, so she instructed all photographers to use a certain new Chinese-made camera called a "Red Flag." The camera was a Leica copy. The only problem was that it didn't work too well, and no one wanted to take the chance of missing pictures of this historic visit. The result? All the photographers wore the Red Flag cameras prominently on their chests but used their Leicas instead.

Li photographs the "revolutionary opera," *Ode to Yimeng Mountain* performed by the Central Ballet Troupe from Beijing in Acheng county, Heilongjiang province, on 23 July 1975. His presence on the stage during a performance of *The White-Haired Girl* later that day elicited criticism from Mao's wife, Jiang Qing (photograph by Wang Hongben).

Jiang Qing was also the cause for one of my most anxious moments during the Cultural Revolution. It happened in July 1975, when I traveled to Acheng county to photograph a performance of the model opera *The White-Haired Girl*, by the Central Ballet Troupe from Beijing. More than fifty thousand people were watching from the slope of a hill, and during the performance I ventured out to the center of the stage to take a picture of two ballet dancers from behind so you could see the crowd. And I got it — this decisive moment. But when I exited the stage, the stage manager was furious. I became very nervous; the production of the ballet had been supervised by Jiang herself, the "flag bearer of revolutionary arts," and the head of the troupe reported directly to her in Beijing every evening by telephone.

That night I went to the deputy director of Heilongjiang's Cultural Bureau that had received the troupe, the composer of "Rely on the Helmsman While Sailing the Seas," Wang Shuangying. Wang was an old friend and promised to help me out. The next morning, he had breakfast with the head of the troupe. Yes, Wang discovered, the head of the troupe had spoken to Madame Mao, and indeed, the Chairman's wife was very upset. She said that my presence on the stage had "sabotaged the revolutionary model opera" by putting an extra character in the show. This was a very serious political accusation. She told the head of the troupe that the reckless photographer must be fired and have his

Party membership revoked. The head of the troupe told Wang he didn't dare fail to carry out instructions from Jiang Qing. Luckily for me, Wang reassured him. "You have reported the incident to me and are no longer responsible. You have done your job. Since the provincial committee asked me to oversee the troupe's visit, let me take it from here. I know how to handle this type of situation."

But bad as she was, personally I don't hold Jiang Qing fully responsible for the excesses of the Cultural Revolution. Really, she was just a thug. "I was Chairman Mao's dog," she once said. "If he told me to bite, I bit."

When I was young and lived in the village in Shandong province, my grandfather helped me with my education. He was my first real teacher. He had a lot of books, and I remember that he started by having me memorize the *Three Character Scripture* — a book of maxims of ancient wisdom all written in three characters. I still recall the first one: "When one is born, one has a kind heart."

The idea behind the saying was this: People's vicious aspects are developed, cultivated; social and political changes can and do alter human nature. That's why I don't think one can attribute an evil spirit to the Red Guards or students. The girls and boys who shaved the head of the governor, for example, were really quite young, just teenagers. I don't think they had vicious natures. They were just following Mao, heeding his call. "Revolution is not a dinner party," he said. "It is a violent act of one class overthrowing another."

My generation had not experienced the purge of the landlords or the anti-rightist campaign in the 1950s. We had been raised by the Communist Party and taught to believe that without Mao, there would be no new China, that he had liberated us from the old society and sought only the happiness and well-being of the people. But he used us. He didn't invoke the old anti–Chiang Kai-shek slogan "It is right to rebel" to win power, but once he already had it. He used it against his own regime, to purge President Liu Shaoqi. That was the real root of the Cultural Revolution.

But if Mao had wanted to purge the president, he didn't need to mobilize the masses to do it. But then if he'd had a more humanitarian thinking, *everything* would have been different, a different China, a different world. Only he forgot his humble peasant background, the very humanity he promoted in his writings, and as a result all China suffered. And in a sense he also suffered. Yes, Mao was a

i in front of Mao's birthplace
f Shaoshan in Hunan province
photograph by Tang Dabai).
June 1972

251

victim of the Cultural Revolution, too; the fire he lit ended up swallowing him as well. By the time he died, most people had realized the Cultural Revolution was a disaster. There is a saying: "One picks up a big rock only to drop it on his own foot." We didn't have any public-opinion polls in China, but if we had, I believe Mao's popularity index would have been quite low by then.

Today, after two decades of reform, people's minds are emancipated. They can think on their own. That wasn't the case then. Then, middle-school students battled one another to the death and jumped off roofs shouting, "Long Live Chairman Mao," rather than surrender. Then, the post office issued a stamp of a heroic "sent down" youth named Jin Xuanhua, who died trying to save an electrical pole in a flooding river — it was brave, but meaningless.

I believe in objective truth, not superstition. Even so, the disastrous events of 1976 seemed particularly portentous. On 28 July, China suffered the worst earthquake in recorded history, which demolished the city of Tangshan in Hebei province and killed a quarter of a million people. And that same year the three major male figures of my life died one after the other: first, our respected leader, Premier Zhou Enlai, who succumbed to cancer on January 8; then my father, who died of heart disease on 19 February; and finally, Mao Zedong, who passed out of this world on 9 September 1976.

Mao was eighty-three, and everyone knew he was dying. In newsreels, we saw him aging, saw saliva dripping down his chin. My friends at the Xinhua News Agency who were sent to the Study of Chrysanthemum Fragrance to take pictures of Mao during the late period told me that no one was allowed to use a flash and that special lights were set up so as not to disturb the eyes of our Leader.

But no one lives forever. Party members were the first to be informed of Mao's death. Then they let the people know through the radio and newspapers. Most people didn't have television sets yet. I myself heard the news at the paper. At that moment I don't remember feeling much of anything.

During Mao's memorial, I deliberately set out to discover if anyone was truly grieving. They played the funeral dirge and created a solemn atmosphere, but I only found one woman in gray with a few teardrops on her coat. But even though she was pretending to be sad and tried to make others believe she was crying, I didn't see any more tears. Then I spotted a model worker I had once interviewed. I said to him, "Master Su, we're all very sad about Chairman Mao's death. How about taking a picture of you crying to show that you really miss him a lot?" He said, "I understand your meaning. Indeed, I'm very sad about the old man's death. In fact, I just shed some tears a moment ago." But then, although I waited for a long time as he tried to squeeze a few more out, he couldn't

The large picture (bottom) was published in the *Heilongjiang Daily* in December 1974 as part of a photo essay devoted to an irrigation project in Shuangcheng county. The site was officially inspected by Liu Guangtao (center, with star on hat), first secretary of the provincial Party committee and director of the provincial revolutionary committee, and his deputy Yang Yichen (to his left). Li was not able to include in a single frame the two dignitaries greeting local Party leaders. The editors asked him to make one image from two frames (below) by cutting and pasting them together. Additional retouching made the scene seem more "real" and upbeat.

do it, and I was only able to take a picture of him wearing a sad expression, without tears.

If you compare the Chinese people's feeling toward Zhou Enlai, you see the difference. When Zhou passed away the Central Committee gave the order not to have a memorial anywhere in China. But in Beijing people took the initiative and created one in Tiananmen Square. Zhou had suffered a lot to try to prevent the disaster from extending too far, and to many he was regarded as nearly perfect. At the newspaper, some former members of the Red Youth Fighting Team and I hung up a picture of him that we had cut from the newspaper. Eventually, the army representative persuaded us to take it down. But most people felt a major pillar of China was lost when Zhou passed away, while with Mao they only said, "He's finally gone."

Li on the phone in his office at the *Heilongjiang Daily* in Harbin (photographed with a self-timer). 5 August 1975

It was the nature of the times that many were forced to do things they were later ashamed of — including myself. In particular, I remember an incident that occurred when I went to Beijing in January 1967 for the debate to decide which was the real rebel group, the time I received the Red-Color News Soldier armband. The meeting took place at the National Headquarters of the Red Rebels in News Media, in a one-story Beijing-style building that ringed a courtyard. In one of the rooms, the representative of the opposing group, Xue Yunfu, and I faced off. Xue was a senior editor in the politics and education department at the paper, ten years older than me, and not a bad person. But at some point during the debate he told the official from the headquarters, "I can pledge with my integrity that we are the real rebel group." This enraged me, and without a second thought I reached into my pocket and pulled out a one-*fen* coin.

"Your integrity is worth less than this *fen*!" I cried out sarcastically. Then, to utterly disgrace him, I threw the coin out the open door into the courtyard. Dumbfounded, Xue blushed and stood speechless, and I felt quite pleased with myself.

After all these years, the memory of that moment still fills me with shame.

I think we must try, through serious reflection, through contemplation, to relieve those whose souls were tortured. I want to show the world what really happened during the Cultural Revolution — how it was a movement in which people were turned against other people in order to survive, how all were victims: those beaten and killed as well as those who inflicted suffering on others. It may be "petty bourgeois" of me, but I think people need kindness and honesty — not just class struggle. There's nothing wrong with revolution, if the objective is to free each person to fulfill their potential. During the Cultural Revolution this was considered "seeking too much success." Publicly, maybe, I agreed; but in reality I always sought success though many — the Red Guards, my superiors, even my colleagues — tried to prevent me. They all thought I was merely someone who didn't want to listen to the Party. But more than thirty years later when you look at the photographs I took, you see the real image of the Cultural Revolution. And it exists for the same reason I was never accepted as a member of the Communist Party: because basically I'm a person with a rebellious nature. I make my own choice according to my own will. And if I achieved something, including these photographs, I would say the reason is that I always believed I should make it by myself.

•

On 6 October 1976, about a month after the death of Mao, the Central Committee of the Party in Beijing headed by Hua Guofeng smashed the Gang of Four. I remember the day the news was formally disclosed very clearly; I was at the newspaper, and I was happy beyond description. We all were. The fall of the Gang of Four meant that the Cultural Revolution was over, the madness at an end. The radical bunch, responsible for so many unconscionable acts, was headed for jail.

That afternoon, the staff of the paper gathered in the cafeteria to celebrate. The mood was euphoric. After ten years of fear and uncertainty, a spontaneous sense of joy overcame us all. We laughed and clapped one another on the back. We made toasts and drank alcohol, and everyone became very emotional. Many people, including myself, got pretty drunk.

By that time, Yingxia and I had already moved into our new apartment, which was quite close to the newspaper, and after work she picked up our daughter Xiaobing from nursery school and met me at the office so we could all walk home together. Xiaobing was four years old at the time and a real beauty. Her nursery-school teacher had nicknamed her *Doudou* — "little bean."

I remember that it was snowing that day. A coating of white powder and ice covered the road. The whole way home, I was dancing. People on the street were laughing at me, but in a friendly way — they knew what it was all about. Then, because it was quite slippery, when we were about a block away from home Yingxia asked me to carry Xiaobing across the street. I picked her up, but

i (left) during the eulogy for Mao by Liu Guangtao, first secretary of the provincial Party committee and director of the provincial revolutionary committee, at the memorial service at People's Stadium in Harbin (photograph by Xu Wanyu). 18 September 1976

Li with his daughter Xiaobing in his office at the *Heilongjiang Daily* (photographed with a self-timer). 12 July 1976

having had too much to drink, I hoisted her up with too much strength and tossed her right over my shoulder.

For an instant, I stood with my arms outstretched in front of me, empty. Then I heard Yingxia scream, and I spun around as Xiaobing flew into the air, did a somersault, and landed on her back in the snow with a thud. Immediately, she began to wail. That sobered me up in a flash. Yingxia and I quickly undid her overcoat and checked her for injuries, but she didn't have a scratch on her — just one last parting gift of terror from the Cultural Revolution.

Yingxia glared at me. "If I had a knife right now, I would *kill* you," she said.

In the years since, Yingxia often reminds Xiaobing about that day. "Doudou," she asks her, "do you remember that time when we were celebrating the fall of the Gang of Four and the end of the Cultural Revolution?"

"Yes," I add laughing, "— that was quite a complicated maneuver you did!"

1972–1976

By 1972, China was adrift between two opposing ideologies, the radical and the rational. On one side was the Chairman's almost universally detested wife, Jiang Qing, the "white-boned demon," promising endless class struggle; on the other stood the long-suffering proponents of modernization and moderation, Zhou Enlai and Deng Xiaoping, offering to end it. The ensuing battle, which contested the very meaning and legacy of the Cultural Revolution, would consume the final four years of Mao Zedong's life.

Lin Biao's betrayal, Richard Nixon's visit, Deng Xiaoping's return to power — which culminated in his taking over responsibility for foreign affairs from the ailing Zhou Enlai in 1974 — and Mao's rebuke to Jiang Qing the same year for forming an ultraleftist clique, the Gang of Four, all suggested a decisive ideological retreat. Yet, significantly, Deng returned to public life only after writing a letter to the Chairman praising the Cultural Revolution and pledging "never to reverse the verdict." Nor did Mao suppress Jiang Qing and the radicals. Jiang continued to set the socialist standard of culture, and the "Anti–Lin Biao, Anti-Confucius" campaign in 1974 — a thinly veiled attack on Zhou Enlai — like the subsequent anti–Deng Xiaoping campaign in 1976, was largely her faction's work. A further swipe at the modernizers was a program training a million "barefoot doctors" in the countryside, in lieu of more modern, Western-style hospitals and specialists.

But while Mao never repudiated radicalism or the Cultural Revolution, neither did he make plans to pass it on to the future. He had grown to detest his wife as power-hungry and dangerous, while his handpicked successor, Hua Guofeng, on the contrary, was a relatively weak and little-known centrist. Hua would leave no doubt about the road China would take after Mao's death. Less than a month later he would authorize the arrest of Jiang Qing, Wang Hongwen, Zhang Chunqiao, and Yao Wenyuan — smashing the Gang of Four and the revolution from which they had sprung.

Harbin, Heilongjiang province, 8 March 1973

Young pioneers in the auditorium
of the North Plaza Hotel welcome
representatives of Heilongjiang's
Conference of Socialism's
Advanced Work Groups and
Model Workers.

By 1973 the chaos of rampaging
rebel factions on the steps outside
the North Plaza Hotel had given
way to organized meetings inside
the auditorium like this one
of Heilongjiang's Conference of
Socialism's Advanced Work Groups
and Model Workers.

Harbin, 8 March 1973

Harbin, 10 March 1973

Leaders of Heilongjiang's revolutionary committee, including the new first Party secretary Liu Guangtau (third from right), receive representatives of the province's Conference of Socialism's Advanced Work Groups and Model Workers at the North Plaza Hotel.

Model worker "ironwoman" Guo
Fenglian visits an air-raid shelter
project in Mudanjiang City (17 March
1973, below). In Inner Mongolia, a
"barefoot doctor" — one of a million
paramedics employed in the leftist's
answer to Western-style hospitals —
visits patients (30 September 1973,
bottom). On a train traveling from
Qiqihar to Beijing, passengers
are led in chanting slogans of the
"anti–Lin Biao, anti-Confucius"
campaign (8 March 1974, opposite).

Harbin, 19 November 1974

In the mid-1970s, behind Mao's promotion of "unity, stability, and development," China set about redressing the economic ruin wrought by the decade of social unrest. Even political enemies — the radicals, represented by Jiang Qing and the Gang of Four, and the moderates, represented by Zhou Enlai and Deng Xiaoping — seemed in agreement about the need for economic renewal. However, the two camps held different views regarding the means. For Zhou Enlai and Deng Xiaoping it meant embracing foreign capital and technology, and with their help, pursuing the "four modernizations" in industry, agriculture, science and technology, and the military. For the radicals it meant revisiting the principles of the Great Leap Forward, reinvigorating the commune system, and increasing production in the spirit of "self-reliance."

Overall the moderates would have the upper hand. The campaign to "criticize revisionism and rectify working style" in 1972 had returned to power many cadres who had been purged for their alleged opposition to the extremist polemics of the Great Leap Forward and the Cultural Revolution, and new agreements with the West in the wake of Richard Nixon's visits to China prompted increased international trade. Yet the radicals would not go silently. Their power rested increasingly on the Chairman's fear that the entire Cultural Revolution, and he himself, would be discredited in the process of liberalization. Now, against the backdrop of Mao's failing health — he would be diagnosed with Lou Gehrig's disease in 1974 — Jiang Qing and her Gang of Four set about reconsolidating their power base, launching new attacks directed against "those in power still taking the capitalist road," and heaping scorn on the "worship for all things Western."

In an effort to redress the economy after a decade of social unrest, Mao slowly opened China to international trade. Here, workers in a Harbin shoe factory discuss the development of new shoe styles to meet market needs.

"Educated youth" and local peasants collaborate to till and irrigate the frozen land in preparation of the season's planting.

Chaoyang commune, Shuangcheng county, 17 December 1974

Handian and Chaoyang communes, Shuangcheng county, 17 December 1974

Peasants break up the frozen
fields of northern Heilongjiang
(opposite), while teams of female
workers are sent to retrieve
cartloads of mud to enrich the
heavily salinated soil.

After a decade of turmoil, the hardship of life in China's rural areas remained largely unchanged. Here a pregnant woman carries frozen clod in the annual mass effort to revitalize the arid land.

Handian commune, Shuangcheng county, 18 December 1974

Peasants and predominantly female "educated youth" from the cities use sandy soil from muddy fields to reduce the saline level of the land and prepare for planting.

Xiqin commune, Shuangcheng county, 19 December 1974

It had been Jiang Qing's orchestrated attacks on the play *The Dismissal of Hairui from Office* that had launched the Cultural Revolution in the mid-1960s, and long after the political power of the ultraleft began to wane, her control over the cultural sphere remained unchallenged. To the extent that the Cultural Revolution was indeed a battle over culture, Jiang Qing fought it to the end.

Central to her purpose were her eight "model operas." Performed for millions throughout China, each was intended as a lesson in the evils of the old society contrasted with the new "realm of red virtue." One of the best known, *The White-Haired Girl,* tells the story of a young peasant, Xier, who flees her evil landlord and for years survives outdoors in blazing summers and icy winters that turn her hair from black to a ghostly white. A stand-in for Jiang Qing herself, Xier in the opera's climax shakes her fist toward heaven and shouts, "I am water that cannot be mopped up, fire that cannot be put down. I shall live! And vengeance is mine!"

Jiang took one last star turn on the political stage after the death of Zhou Enlai in 1976 sparked a spontaneous memorial in Beijing. On 5 April tens of thousands of people defied a national order and poured into Tiananmen Square to build a shrine of wreaths at the monument to the People's Unknown Hero. An implicit criticism of Mao and the policies of the Cultural Revolution, the event was ascribed to an "anti-deviationist wind" and blamed on Deng Xiaoping, who was stripped of his position two days later. Jiang helped organize the anti-Deng campaign that inevitably followed, but her victory would be short-lived. The new Party chairman, Hua Guofeng, ordered her arrest along with the rest of the Gang of Four three weeks after Mao's death. Jiang narrowly evaded execution and spent the next fifteen years in prison. In 1991, at the age of seventy-seven and suffering from cancer, she hanged herself, like so many of her victims before her.

Ballet version of *The Red Women Troop,* one of Jiang Qing's eight "model operas," performed by the National Ballet Company of Beijing.

Daqing, 20 July 1975

Acheng and Shangzhi counties, 23 July–1 September 1975

The National Ballet Company of
Beijing performs *The White-Haired
Girl*, one of Jiang Qing's eight
"model operas," for the local
farmers and peasants of Yuquan
commune (opposite). A young girl
of China's Korean minority
is sent airborne from a seesaw
during the county's annual games
in Hedong commune (above).

"Educated youth" and local peasants of the Xingan production brigade work on an arid field's terrace irrigation system.

Xinsheng commune, Baiquan county, 10 November 1975

An all-female militia squad
patrols the snow-covered Hufeng
forestry center approximately
120 kilometers southeast of Harbin.

Shangzhi county, 16 February 1976

Harbin, 9 April 1976

Following Mao's decision to
remove Deng Xiaoping from all
public positions — holding him
accountable for the spontaneous
and unsanctioned memorials
after Zhou Enlai's death — PLA
soldiers assemble in Harbin's
People's Stadium (formerly Red
Guard Square) with banners that
"indignantly denounce the crimes
of Deng Xiaoping."

Hedong commune, Shangzhi county, and Daqing, 18–22 June 1976

Economic reconstruction involved both traditional agriculture and modern industry. Here, peasants of China's Korean minority sow rice seedlings (opposite), while scientists at the Daqing research center conduct experiments to increase output from China's largest oil field (below).

A studio photographer from the county capital uses an 8x10 bellows camera to make the official group picture of "educated youth" at Yinlonghe farm, where the "Youth Shock Brigade" (as indicated on flag) participate in building a small dam to regulate irrigation.

Beian county, 25 June 1976

"The Central Committee of the Communist Party of China, the Standing Committee of the National People's Congress of the People's Republic of China, the State Council of the People's Republic of China and the Military of the Communist Party of China announce with deepest grief to the whole Party, the whole army and the people of all nationalities throughout the country:

Comrade Mao Zedong, the esteemed and beloved great leader of our Party, our army and the people of all nationalities of our country, the great teacher of the international proletariat and the oppressed people, Chairman of the Central Committee of the Communist Party of China, Chairman of the Military Commission of the Central Committee of the Communist Party of China, and Honorary Chairman of the National Committee of the Chinese People's Political Consultative Conference, passed away at 00:10 hours, September 9, 1976, in Beijing because of the worsening of his illness and despite all treatment, although meticulous medical care was given him in every way after he fell ill."

Official announcement of the death of Mao Zedong distributed world-wide by the Xinhua News Agency on 9 September 1966.

Five days after Mao's death,
workers in Harbin's Arts and Crafts
Factory make commemorative
wreaths in preparation for the
city's official memorial.

Harbin, 14 September 1976

On 15 September, Party officials fill the mourning hall at the office building of Heilongjiang's Party committee (below). The next day, Leng Pengfei, a hero in the Zhenbao Island battle in the Wusuli River, leads PLA troops in a march to mourn Mao's death (opposite top). A woman sheds a tear in People's Stadium during the official memorial on 18 September (opposite bottom).

Harbin, 15–18 September 1976

Crowds enter Harbin's People's Stadium to attend the city's memorial service for Mao. The billboards read: "Pursue Mao's last will: Carry on the work of the proletarian revolution to the end" (left) and "The Great Leader and teacher Chairman Mao Zedong will live in our hearts forever" (right).

Harbin, 18 September 1976

Hundreds of thousands gather
in Harbin's People's Stadium to
mourn Chairman Mao.

Harbin, 18 September 1976

Harbin, 18 September 1976

Compared with the spontaneous outpouring of mourning that erupted following Zhou Enlai's death half a year earlier, or with the exuberant rejoicing upon the arrest of the Gang of Four soon to come, Mao Zedong's death elicited a subdued reaction. After years of turmoil, the revolutionary hero and founder of modern China was viewed as neither god nor myth, but simply as an all-too-human leader for whom reverence had largely eroded.

But Mao would not undergo the public criticism that followed the death of Joseph Stalin in the Soviet Union, in part because in China there was no way to separate Mao from the Communist Party — Mao *was* the Party. Similarly, there was no way to separate the Party from the Cultural Revolution it had helped to unleash. The result was a nation of silent accomplices and victims, often both at the same time. Quietly, scores of purged cadres would be returned to power over the following years, many rehabilitated by Deng Xiaoping, who took power in 1977.

Deng, who had been purged three times and repeatedly criticized and humiliated, was in the strongest position to discredit Mao, but he never did. The Cultural Revolution, however, was a different matter. While the Central Committee continued to insist that Mao's mistakes were "secondary, his merits primary," in June 1981 the 11th Party Congress issued a historic resolution that held: "Practice has shown that the 'cultural revolution' did not in fact constitute a revolution or social progress in any sense. . . . Chief responsibility for the grave error of the Cultural Revolution, an error comprehensive in magnitude and protracted in duration, does indeed lie with Comrade Mao Zedong. In his later years . . . far from making a correct analysis of many problems, he confused right and wrong and the people with the enemy. . . . Herein lies his tragedy."

During Mao's memorial, provincial Party leaders, some of whom had been denounced at the height of the Cultural Revolution, pay their respects to the deceased leader. From left to right: Wang Yilun (with bald head), Yu Hongliang, Ren Zhongyi, Liu Guangtao, Zhang Lianchi, Yang Yichen, Li Lian, You Haoyang, Xia Guangya, and Li Jianbai.

In People's Stadium, half a million
people celebrate the "great victory
of smashing the Gang of Four's
conspiracy to usurp the power
of the leadership and the Party"
(on banner above) and the end
of the Cultural Revolution.

Harbin, 23 October 1976

EPILOGUE

Following the death of Mao and arrest of the Gang of Four in the fall of 1976, the Cultural Revolution, which had implicated millions of people at every level of society, many of whom remained in power, was encased in an icy silence. One notable exception was the 1979 publication of "People or Monsters?" an expose on a fifty-two-year-old woman named Wang Shouxin, Party branch secretary and manager of the Bin County Coal Company in Heilongjiang province, accused of embezzling an estimated hundred thousand dollars. A lowly cashier before the revolution, Wang formed a rebel group and rode the revolutionary tide to power, later consolidating her control over the entire county through an elaborate network of personal alliances created behind the smoke screen of radical politics.

Written by a formerly denounced journalist, Liu Binyan, "People or Monsters?" brought the "coal queen" of Bin county to national attention. Viewed by some as symptomatic of the influence peddling and graft that permeated the entire country, the case revealed how, long after the slogan shouting of the Cultural Revolution had died away, the conduits of power it created often remained in place, resulting in an entirely new level of authority: those who received power through revolution, then exploited it through personal connections.

The famous trial of the "greatest embezzler since the founding of new China" thrust Heilongjiang province once more into the public spotlight. Following a three-day open trial in Harbin, Wang was found guilty. Her death sentence, seen by many as excessive in light of the violence systematically perpetrated by others during the same period, was pronounced and carried out in February 1980.

Harbin, 8 February 1980

Wang Shouxin, a former rebel and
Party branch secretary during
the Cultural Revolution, is hauled
before a crowd of five thousand
"guests" at Harbin's Workers Arena
to hear her sentence on charges
of embezzlement.

To stop Wang from proclaiming her
innocence, the bailiffs dislocate
her jaw (below) before transporting
her by truck to a snowy field on the
rural outskirts of Harbin (opposite
and following pages).

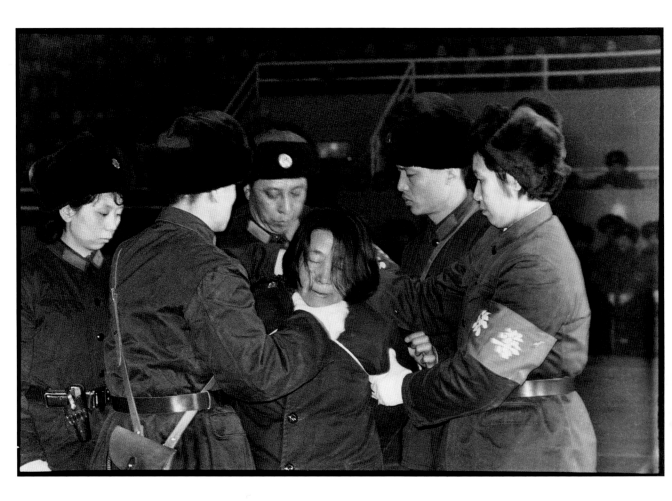

Harbin, 8 February 1980

Wang Shouxin is unloaded onto a
snowy field thirty kilometers
southeast of Harbin and waits for
her sentence to be carried out.

Outskirts of Harbin, 8 February 1980

Outskirts of Harbin, 8 February 1980

Chronology

1911	Overthrow of the Qing dynasty that had been in power since 1644. Sun Yatsen proclaims a provisional republican government on 10 October. Mao Zedong joins the insurrectional army.
1912	Foundation of the Chinese Nationalist Party (Guomindang).
1914	The First World War breaks out in June.
1915	Japan seizes Qingdao, a German colony in China.
1917	China joins the allies in the First World War. (October): Bolshevik Revolution in Russia.
1918	(November): First World War ends. Mao Zedong receives a diploma from the Teacher's College of Hunan province, where he was born on 26 December 1893.
1921	Foundation of the Chinese Communist Party (CCP) in Shanghai with Mao Zedong as secretary.
1921-22	China regains sovereignty over Shandong, a German concession given to Japan by the Treaty of Versailles in 1919.
1922	(September): Miners' strike in Anyuan (Hunan) orchestrated by Mao Zedong. Zhou Enlai forms the Revolutionary Youth League in Paris.
1925	Joseph Stalin becomes the successor to Vladimir Lenin, who died in 1924. (March): Death of Sun Yatsen.
1926	Mao writes *Analysis of the Classes in Chinese Society*.
1927	Chiang Kai-shek crushes the communists in Shanghai.
1928	Creation of the first "soviets" and the first elements of the "Red Army" in the southern provinces by Mao and Zhu De.
1930	Yang Kaihui, Mao's first wife, and Mao's younger sister are beheaded by the nationalists in Changsha (Hunan).
1931	Sino-Japanese crisis over Manchuria. Mao becomes Chairman of the Chinese Soviet Republic, which includes only three provinces (Heilongjiang, Jilin, and Liaoning).
1932	Japanese occupation of Shanghai. Japan creates the puppet government of Manchukuo, headed by the former emperor of China, Pu Yi, inheritor of the Manchu Dynasty.
1934-35	The Red Army carries out the Long March from the provinces of Hunan and Jiangxi to the province of Shaanxi in the north with Zhou Enlai, Zhu De, Lin Biao, Deng Xiaoping and Liu Shaoqi under the leadership of Mao Zedong.
1935	Mao establishes a communist base at Yanan (Shanxi). He Zichen, Mao's second wife, undergoes treatment for cancer in Moscow. Mao meets Jiang Qing and divorces He Zichen. His older brother Mao Zitan is killed in combat at the end of the Long March. (December): Student revolt against the Japanese in Peking.
1937	(December): Japanese army enters the city of Nanjing (Jiangsu), headquarters of the communist government. Nationalists and communists unite against the invaders.
1939	The Second World War breaks out. In August, Hitler and Stalin sign a non-aggression pact. Jiang Qing becomes Mao's third wife.
1940	(August 21): Birth of Li Zhensheng in Dalian (Liaoning).
1941	Pearl Harbor in Hawaii is attacked by Japan. The US enters the Second World War. China declares war on Japan, Germany, and Italy.
1943	Mao Zemin, Mao's younger brother, is executed by the nation Guomindang.
1945	(8 May): Germany capitulates, putting an end to the Second World War. (August): US drops two atomic bombs on the Japanese cities of Hiroshima and Nagasaki, leading to Japan's surrender and the return of Taiwan to China.
1947	(May): Mao's Red Army fights the forces of Chiang Kai-shek. Led by Lin Biao, the Red Army wins an important victory at Jilin. (December): The Red Army becomes the People's Liberation Army (PLA).
1949	(September): Li Zhenli, older half brother of Li Zhensheng, voluntarily joins the communists and is killed at the age of seventeen. Li is brought to Roncheng (Shandong), his family's ancestral home. (1 October): Proclamation of the People's Republic of China; Mao becomes President of the Chinese Communist Party, Head of State and Chairman of the Central Committee Military Commission. Zhou Enlai is appointed Prime Minister. Chiang Kai-shek takes refuge in Taiwan. (December): During his first trip abroad, Mao meets Joseph Stalin in Moscow, where he stays for two months.
1950-53	The Korean War.
1950	Li Zhensheng returns to Dalian. (14 February): Mao and Stalin sign a treaty of friendship, alliance, and mutual assistance between China and the USSR. Marriage and agrarian legislation adopted in China. (September): A contingent of the UN debarks in Korea, followed by the first Chinese volunteers to the North in October. (October): Chinese invasion of Tibet. (25 October): Mao Anying, Mao's oldest son, dies in Korea.
1952	First hydrogen bomb test in the US.
1953	(March): Stalin, Chairman of the Council of the People's Commissars of the USSR, dies.
1954	Geneva Accords: End of the French presence in Indochina. Nikita Khrushchev goes to Beijing for the first time.
1955	Zhou Enlai represents China at the Afro-Asiatic Conference of twenty-nine non-aligned countries in Bandung, Indonesia.
1956	Li Zhensheng attends High School in Dalian, and begins taking photographs. (February): The XXth Congress of the Soviet Communist Party denounces "cult of personality." (May): Hundred Flowers Campaign in China. (September): VIIIth Congress of the CCP; Deng Xiaoping becomes General Secretary of the Central Committee and criticizes the USSR.
1957	The Hundred Flowers is extended by an "anti-rightist" campaign of "rectification." (4 October): The USSR launches Sputnik, the Earth's first artificial satellite. (November): Nikita Khrushchev greets Mao Zedong in Moscow. This is his second and last trip abroad.

1958	The Great Leap Forward: Creation of agricultural communes.

1959   Failure of the Great Leap Forward; famine ravages the country.
(March): Chinese authorities put down the rebellion in Tibet.
The Dalai Lama flees to India.
(April): Liu Shaoqi becomes President of China.
(1 October): After a trip to the US, Nikita Khrushchev
arrives at Beijing for his second and last visit to China.

1960   Li Zhensheng enters the Film School of Changchun (Jilin).
Lin Biao releases the Little Red Book for use as a handbook
by the PLA.
(April): Student riots (125 dead and 1,000 wounded)
in South Korea; President Syngman Rhee resigns.
(July): The USSR recalls all its advisors from China.

1961   China is strongly criticized at the XXIInd Congress of
the Communist Party of the Soviet Union. Zhou Enlai leaves
Moscow; breaking-off between the two countries.
(13 August): The German Democratic Republic (GDR) erects
the Berlin Wall, which will remain in place until 1989.

1962   The Film School of Changchun is converted into a School of
Photojournalism.
Socialist Education Movement in rural China.
Crisis between the USSR and the US over Soviet missiles
installed in Cuba. Khruschev pulls them back in October.

1963   Li finds a job in the photography department of the
Heilongjiang Daily newspaper in Harbin (Heilongjiang).
(22 November): John F. Kennedy, president of the United
States, is assassinated in Dallas, Texas.
Zhou Enlai visits several African countries.

1964   (27 January): Recognition of the People's Republic of China
by President Charles de Gaulle of France.
(October): Li Zhensheng goes to the countryside as part of
the Socialist Education Movement.
(16 October): First test of the Chinese atomic bomb.

1965   American President Lyndon Johnson sends troops to South
Vietnam. Intensive aerial bombing in the North.

1966   (16 May): Official start of the Great Proletarian Cultural
Revolution in China.
(16 July): Mao Zedong swims in the Yangtze
(5 August): Mao writes his dazibao, "Bombard the
Headquarters."
(18 August): Mao Zedong receives the Red Guard in
Tiananmen Square in Peking (Beijing) for the first time.
(Autumn): Li Zhensheng creates the "Red Youth Fighting
Team" at his newspaper.

1967   (January): The Cultural Revolution reaches the army.
(April): President Liu Shaoqi is accused of fomenting a coup
against Mao in January 1966; attacks against "bourgeois" and
"revisionists."
(May): Serious incident involving the People's Liberation Army
and the Red Guards in Beijing and in other cities of the
country.
(17 June): Explosion of China's first hydrogen bomb.
(August): The Eighth Central Committee of the CCP approves
the Cultural Revolution and the economic policy of Mao.
(Summer): Insurrections in some cities and provinces,
particularly in Wuhan (Hubei)
(October): Pu Yi, the last emperor of China, dies in Beijing.

1968   (January): The American spy ship, the *Pueblo*, is captured by
North Korean forces.
(May): Student uprisings and general strike in Paris.
(20 August): The Prague Spring is put down by the Soviets.
(October): Birth of Xiaohan, son of Li Zhensheng.
The CCP officially proclaims the end of the Great Proletarian
Cultural Revolution.

(26 December): Li Zhensheng is publicly accused of being
a "newly born bourgeois" and a "foreign agent."

1969   (April): The IXth Congress of the CCP names Lin Biao as
Mao's successor when the Chairman decides to retire.
(July): Americans Buzz Aldrin and Neil Armstrong walk on the
moon.
(6 September): Li is sent to the Liuhe May 7th Cadre School
for reeducation.
(November): Death of Liu Shaoqi, made public five years later.

1970   Coup by General Lon Nol in Cambodia. Prince Norodom
Sihanouk is overthrown. He lives in exile in Beijing.

1971   (September): Failed attempt to overthrow Mao; Lin Biao
leaves for the USSR; his plane crashes in Mongolia.
(October): The People's Republic of China replaces Taiwan
at the United Nations.

1972   Rehabilitated, Li Zhensheng is appointed director of the
photo department of the *Heilongjiang Daily*.
(February): Birth of Xiaobing, the daughter of Li Zhensheng.
(February): Meeting between Mao and American President
Richard Nixon.
Establishment of diplomatic relations between China and the
United Kingdom, followed by the Federal Republic of
Germany.

1973   (January): Confrontation of factions within the Chinese
Communist Party between radicals led by Mao's wife Jiang
Qing and moderates like Zhou Enlai and Deng Xiaoping.
(April): Deng, protégé of Zhou, is appointed Vice Prime
Minister.
(16 September): President Georges Pompidou of France
meets Mao in Beijing.

1974   (August): In the United States, Richard Nixon resigns
following the Watergate scandal.
Portraits of Mao painted by Andy Warhol in 1972 are exhibited
for the first time (Galliéra Museum in Paris).

1975   (April): Death of Chiang Kai-shek in Taiwan.
(17 April): The Khmer Rouge enter Phnom Penh.
(30 April): The Vietnamese communist forces enter Saigon;
the Vietnam War ends.
(December): Official visit to China by the American President
Gerald Ford, who meets with Mao.

1976   (8 January): Death of Zhou Enlai.
(February): Death of Li Zhensheng's father, Li Yuanjian.
(April): Hua Guofeng succeeds Zhou as Prime Minister.
(28 July): Between 250,000 and 750,000 persons die in an
earthquake at Tangshang, southeast of Beijing.
(9 September): Death of Mao Zedong.
(6 October): Hua orders the arrest of the Band of Four (Jang
Qing, Yao Wenyuan, Zhang Chunqiao and Wang Hongwen),
marking the historic end of the Cultural Revolution.
Hua succeeds Mao at the head of the Chinese Communist
Party.

1977   Deng Xiaoping is rehabilitated.

1978   Deng is appointed Vice Prime Minister at the head of the
Military Affairs Commission from 1981 to 1989. He launches
economic modernization and the "open door" policy.

1979   (1 January): Diplomatic relations with the United States are
officially reestablished.
(28 January): Official visit of Deng Xiaoping to the US under
the presidency of Jimmy Carter.

1980   Li Zhensheng begins teaching photography in the journalism
department of University Beijing's International Political
Science Institute.

Acknowledgements:

This book is dedicated to the fallen of the Cultural Revolution, and all who blazed through its storms.

Red-Color News Soldier was many years in the making and involved the efforts of dozens all over the world.

My foremost thanks to the book's contributors:
Robert Pledge, who conceived and edited this multi-dimensional project, and meticulously saw it through every stage of development since we first began planning it in 1988.
Jacques Menasche, who gave this book a voice with nearly thirty-thousand words based on three years of historical research and hundreds of hours of in-depth interviews.
Jiang Rong, whose translations provided the bridge between two very different cultures, and without whose coordination this book would never have come about.
Li Xiaobing, who greatly assisted in the research and translations, especially in relation to the detailed captions, and who also happens to be my daughter.
Jonathan Spence, professor at Yale University, who offered the eloquent and thoughtful introduction.
Zhang Aiping, former vice-premier and defense minister, who wrote the calligraphy for the front piece and whose early support first led me to believe that such a book was indeed possible.
All those at Contact Press Images, especially Dominique Deschavanne who coordinated the French aspects of the project in Paris, and Tim Mapp in New York, who overcame all technical dilemmas of printing and scanning of the images. Also, Jeffrey Smith, Franck Seguin, Nancy Koch, Samantha Box for their assistance throughout the book's production.
All those at Phaidon, notably editors Karen Stein and Valérie Vago-Laurer for their stamina and patience; and Julia Hasting for her beautiful design. Also, Amanda Renshaw and publisher Richard Schlagman, whose enthusiasm and belief in this work were never in doubt.
Peter Wang (Wang Gang), president of Redstone Images, who scanned the photographs with dedication and sometimes with the help of my son Li Xiaohan.
Carma Hinton, independent filmmaker, founder and director of the Long Bow Group, Nancy Hearst, librarian of the Fairbank Center for East Asian research at Harvard University, and Professor Geremie R. Barmé, of The Australian National University, who offered detailed historical advice on text and captions.
Guo Cunfa, deputy director of the Photographic Center of the *Heilongjiang Daily* Enterprise Group in Harbin, who provided significant items on the Cultural Revolution from the newspaper I worked for.
Gabriel Bauret, Joe Regal, Li Shi, Liu Xin, Liao Bilan, Tal Halevi, Zohra Mokhtari, and Zuo Cui provided useful advice and support at many moments throughout this project.
Wan Jiyao, Xu Wanyu, Liu Qixiang, Wang Hongben, Liu Guoqi, Xin Hua, all photographers who contributed their pictures of me.

For those teachers and friends in China who long ago shaped my life:
Wu Yingxian, my mentor, who told me in 1961: "A photojournalist is not only a witness to history, but should also be a recorder of history."
Ge Weiqing, my teacher and a film artist, who told me: "Only when you have turned the difficulties into driving forces of your life, can you reach the climax of your career."
And also: Xing Shinliang, Lin Xianjuan, Liu Wenshan, Dong Jigang, Zhang Shouyu for their most sincere understanding and friendship.

Finally, I wish to acknowledge my family:
Li Xingcun, my grandfather and my first teacher, who gave me the name "Zhensheng"; Li Yuanjian, my father, who supported me in finishing my studies at the film school despite many difficulties; Chen Shilan, my biological mother, who gave life to me and to my sister, but passed away when I was only three years old; Wang Shuying, my stepmother, who raised my sister and I as her own, and looked after my infant son when my wife and I were "sent down" to the May 7th Cadre School; Zu Shoushan, my father-in-law, who agreed to let me marry his daughter without even meeting me, and committed suicide during the Cultural Revolution; Zu Guanshi, my mother-in-law, who came to Harbin when my son was just born to care for my wife, despite the fact that her husband had been persecuted to death not long before; Li Zhenli, my stepbrother, who joined Mao's army at the age of sixteen and died during the War of Liberation; Li Shufang, my sister, who took care of my elderly parents for many years so I could concentrate on my studies and work; my son, Li Xiaohan, who along with my daughter, Li Xiaobing, helped me sort out my materials and photographs; and most importantly, my wife, Zu Yingxia, who accompanied me in blazing the storms of the Cultural Revolution. Over the past thirty-five years of our marriage, she has always given me the most sincere and unselfish understanding and support.

I would like to thank all those who gave me their sincere love and encouragement, which has been the driving force of my life. I would also like to thank those who hated me and prevented my success out of jealousy. Because of their attacks and suppression, I grew stronger in times of difficulty.

The list of the people who have helped me is too long to be exhaustive.

•

Li Zhensheng born in 1940 in China; graduated from the Changchun Film School in Jilin; joined the *Heilongjiang Daily* as a photojournalist; in October 1964, sent to the countryside as part of the Socialist Education Movement. Returned to Harbin in March 1966, before the start of the Cultural Revolution; in December 1969, sent to the Liuhe May 7th Cadre School for "reeducation"; back at the newspaper in 1971 as head of the photo department; in 1982, in charge of the photography at the journalism department of Beijing's International Political Science Institute; currently engaged in research and writing.

Robert Pledge born in 1942 in England, raised in France; started as a journalist specialized in African affairs; co-founded Contact Press Images in New York in 1976; originated and curated numerous exhibitions, such as *Contact: Photo-journalism Since Vietnam* in 1987, the first contemporary Western photojournalism exhibit in the People's Republic of China.

Jacques Menasche born in 1964 in the USA; NYU graduate; journalist; his first-hand account of September 11 appeared in *NewYorkSeptemberElevenTwoThousandandOne* (2001); reported for the *New York Daily News* on the 2001 war in Afghanistan.

Jonathan D. Spence born in 1936 in England; Professor of History at Yale University in the USA; one of the world's foremost experts on China, he is the author of landmark books including *The Search for Modern China* (1990) and *Mao Zedong* (2002).

Zhang Aiping (calligraphy) born in 1910 in China; took part in the Long March with Mao; made general in 1955; oversaw China's nuclear program; denounced during the Cultural Revolution and spent five years in prison; vice-premier and defense minister under Deng Xiaoping.

Jiang Rong (translation) born in China in 1962; graduated from Shanghai University of Foreign Studies in 1982; since 1989 has worked at the United Nations headquarters in New York as a translator.

Li Xiaobing (research and translation) born in 1972 in China; graduate in journalism at Renmin University in Beijing; currently works in New York City.

Phaidon Press Limited

Regent's Wharf

All Saints Street

London N1 9PA

Phaidon Press Inc.

180 Varick Street

New York, NY 10014

www.phaidon.com

First published 2003

© 2003 Phaidon Press Limited

ISBN 0 7148 4308 3

A CIP catalogue record for this book is available from the
British Library.

All rights reserved. No part of this publication may be reproduced,
stored in a retrieval system or transmitted, in any form or by any
means, electronic, mechanical, photocopying, recording or other-
wise, without the written permission of Phaidon Press Limited.

Designed by Julia Hasting

Printed in Italy